THE ART OF MASS EFFECT

Prima Games
A Division of Random House, Inc.

3000 Lava Ridge Court, Suite 100
Roseville, CA 95661
www.primagames.com

Product Manager: Mario De Govia
Editor: Brooke Hall
Manufacturing: Stephanie Sanchez
Design and Layout: José de Jesús Ramírez

BioWare Corp.:

Mass Effect Project Director
Casey Hudson

Mass Effect Art Director
Derek Watts

Microsoft Game Studios:

Executive Producer
Jorg Neumann

Art Director
Tim Dean

ISBN: 978-0-7615-5851-4
Library of Congress Catalog Card Number: 2006904297
Printed in the United States of America

07 08 09 10 LL 10 9 8 7 6 5 4 3 2 1

TABLE OF CONTENTS

It's not easy building a universe. In fact, we invested a good portion of Mass Effect's several hundred man-years of development into defining the galaxy of life-forms, technologies, and locations that would provide the setting for this epic videogame. As intimidating as that was, it was made even more difficult by the stunning level of detail that would be made possible by the coming generation of hardware and software. Art concepts would now have to consider complex material properties, subtleties in lighting and shadow, and details as fine as individual pores on an alien's skin. For the first time, a videogame had the potential to rival the visual quality and cinematic drama of a live-action motion picture. With that in mind, we set forth on a journey that would not only challenge the limits of our creativity, but also our ability to transform the fruits of our imagination into a believable reality.

The process began with more questions than answers. We asked ourselves some fundamental questions about what "space adventure" really meant to us. In an ideal space adventure, what would we want to do? Where would we want to go? What amazing things would we hope to see there? Our earliest ideas came from things that inspired us in our youth: the exploits of real-life astronauts, spectacular paintings that adorned science-fiction book covers, and the movies of the late 70s and early 80s that immersed us in thickly atmospheric visions of the future.

From that starting point, we began to resolve a clear vision for the art style of Mass Effect. It would be a seemingly idyllic future—a bright universe, with the darkest of secrets. The civilizations of the galaxy would enjoy architecture and vehicles of elegant beauty, making use of simple geometry: compass arcs intersecting straight lines to create shapes that seemed to result from engineering as much as from art. And we would carefully age and weather their surfaces to anchor them in a realistic setting.

Free of the limitations of conventional cinema, where alien costumes often need to fit over the form of a human actor, we explored the full range of possibilities for alien anatomy. But as wild as some of the ideas were, we knew that each of our alien characters had to be capable of projecting the human emotion that would give impact to their part of story. Therefore they would not only have to look plausible as living creatures, but they would need physical features and movements that would allow them to realistically express a range of emotions.

And to pull it all together in a unified visual style, we added a soft, film-like quality to the rendering of the game. As in real-life photography, we would use depth-of-field effects to focus on a character's face, against a softly blurred background. Light would bloom from brightly-lit edges, and a subtle vignetting effect would darken the corners of the image, as though the scene had been filmed with real cameras and projected in a theatre. Finally, a light film grain was introduced to lend a soft analog feel to an otherwise harsh digital image.

In the role of Director, it was my honor to work with a tremendously talented team of artists who spent several years realizing this challenging vision. The requirements of our storyline frequently offered a new aspect of the universe to design, and Art Director Derek Watts and I would discuss ideas for direction. In turn, Derek and his concept artists quickly produced a multitude of images that each visualized our thoughts in exciting new ways. Then, as a team of artists and writers, we would springboard off of great ideas and infuse them with new twists as we moved towards final designs. Once approved, the final concept would then be meticulously sculpted as a 3D model, painted with a complex layering of materials, and then brought to life through the most advanced programming and animation methods we had ever developed. Most satisfying of all, these complex art pieces ultimately came together to immerse players in a single picture: a living, breathing vision of the future.

The art in this book reveals how this process resulted in the imagery you see in the game, including the wealth of compelling artwork that represents the steps made along the way. We hope you enjoy it.

—Casey Hudson, Project Director, Mass Effect

HEROES AND VILLAINS

With an intense focus on capturing the human emotion of its powerful story, Mass Effect™ required a cast of digital actors of unprecedented realism. Much like the cast of a major motion picture, the detailed appearances of Mass Effect's digital actors would have to capture the very spirit of their characters. For humans, the concepting stage led to the casting of real-life models that were scanned to create 3-D models of their characters' faces. Alien characters, however, had to be meticulously hand-sculpted by artists at BioWare®. In either case, these characters would ultimately go through a process to add dynamic wrinkles, eye movements, and facial expressions, turning them into beings that live and breathe inside a futuristic universe.

01

MAIN HUMAN CHARACTERS

In early sketches of Ashley (1), Kaidan (2), Captain Anderson (3), and Joker (4), BioWare artists explored archetypal ideas about the character's appearances. Joker, the starship Normandy's confident pilot, was originally meant to look sickly, but he was ultimately given a more muscular build. Though these concepts were highly stylized, they gave each character an iconic look that would enable the casting of real-life human models.

EARLY PROMOTIONAL SHOTS OF COMMANDER SHEPARD

The first images of Commander Shepard put him in white armor, which didn't fully capture his character. The "N7" suit was designed to portray Shepard's experience more accurately. The final version, with its darker, weathered material represents Shepard's experience and gritty determination, while its scarlet stripe symbolizes human blood–something he would be willing to sacrifice, when needed.

MATRIARCH BENEZIA

The Matriarch's appearance was designed to capture the beauty and mystical power of the asari, while bearing the dark and mysterious qualities that helped associate her with Saren.

TATTOOS

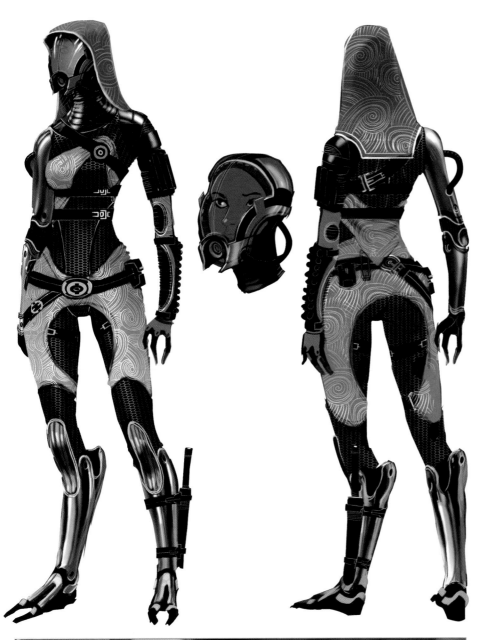

TALI'ZORAH NAR RAYYA AND LIARA

As the sole quarian in Mass Effect, Tali (top) embodies her species' nomadic spirit. Though this concept shows a glimpse of what her face might look like under her visor, her true appearance is never revealed. Liara's face (bottom) did not have a specific design, but rather it was based on original concepts for the asari.

GARRUS

Numerous ideas for facial patterns were evaluated (top) before settling on Garrus' final appearance (bottom).

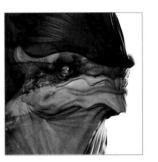

WREX

A fiery red pattern was chosen for Wrex's skull plate, creating a unique and menacing appearance. A deep scar cuts across his face, implying that he survived a near-fatal assault.

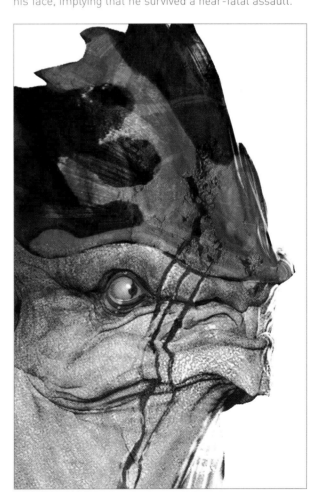

SAREN

Initial concepts of Saren's costume relied on robes and cloaks to lend mystery to his appearance. As Saren's background as a rogue Spectre was developed, however, a more armored appearance was created, one appropriate for an elite turian soldier.

SAREN

A very early concept of Saren (top) and promo-tional images taken of his near-final design (bottom).

SAREN

This painting was developed to help visualize Saren's personality and wardrobe ideas. In several early concepts, Saren carried a cane or sword, providing opportunities for a unique acting performance.

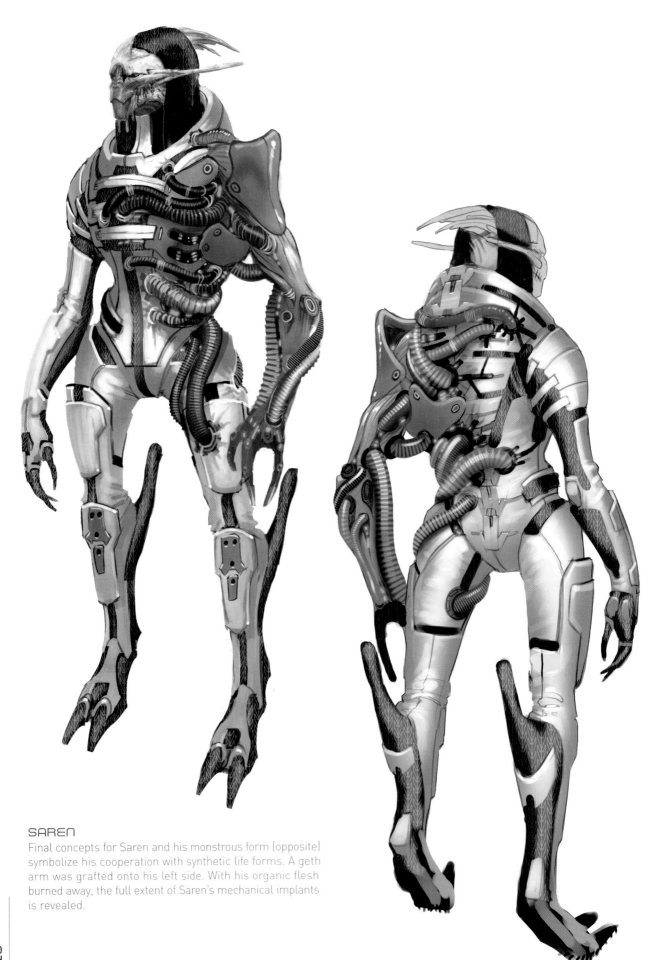

SAREN

Final concepts for Saren and his monstrous form (opposite) symbolize his cooperation with synthetic life forms. A geth arm was grafted onto his left side. With his organic flesh burned away, the full extent of Saren's mechanical implants is revealed.

LIFE-FORMS

To add life to the worlds of Mass Effect, a galaxy of new creatures and aliens was required. To achieve a truly alien appearance for creatures and monsters, artists combined the features of earthly animals in strange combinations, creating unique new creatures with immediately recognizable traits. In addition to these basic life-forms, players would meet characters from advanced alien civilizations that would need to interact with the intelligence and emotion of a human being. Developing the anatomy and costuming of these aliens would require an extensive concepting process, as well as considerable reference to earthly cultures and creatures.

02

ASARI

To capture a familiar element of science fiction "fantasy" fulfillment, one of the main species in Mass Effect was to be a race of beautiful "green alien girls". An extensive exploration of ideas was needed to make them appear exotic and alien while still retaining human qualities allowing them to be desirable as potential love interests.

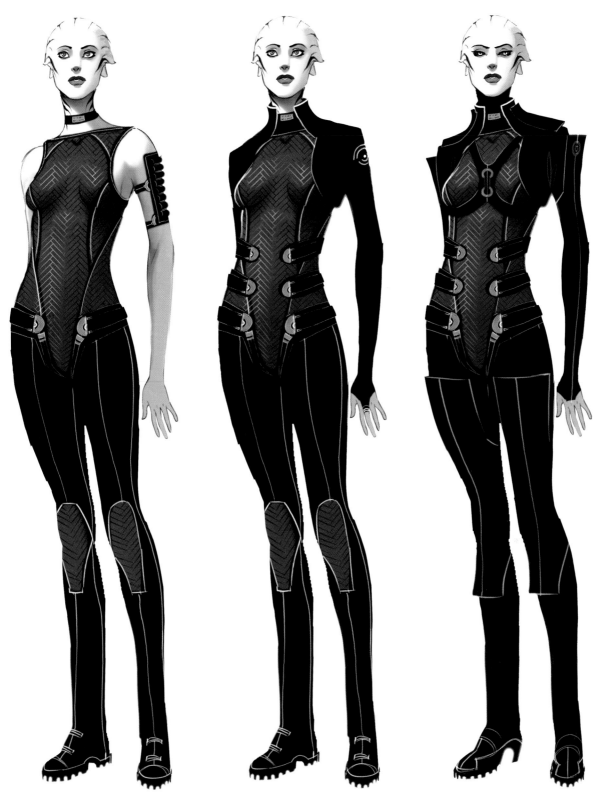

ASARI

Though they are able to wear clothing and armor meant for human females, special costumes were designed for the asari, ranging from the tight-fitting armor of the biotic commandos to the alluring clothing of the asari Consorts.

ASARI

In developing an alien species, it is as important to visualize personality and spirit as much as anatomical details. These paintings helped to define the strength and mystery behind the asari.

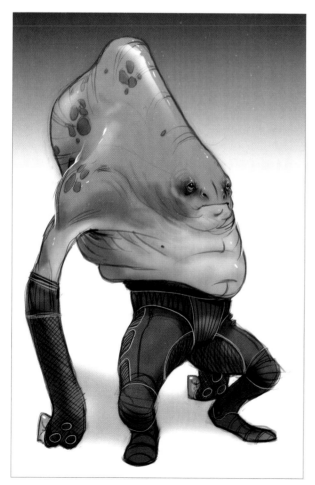

ELCOR

To create additional species to expand and diversify the populations of Mass Effect, BioWare's artists were free to explore countless ideas for weird and wonderful creatures. From this wealth of creativity, the elcor, volus, and hanar were chosen to become three distinctly different species.

ELCOR

The stout and powerful appearance of this concept became a front-runner for the elcor, but its bipedal stance was considered too human.

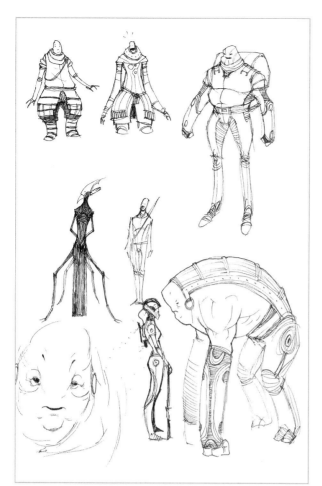

ELCOR

This painting (right) and its original sketch (above) cemented the design for the elcor. They also provided a definitive (and humorous) perspective on their personality.

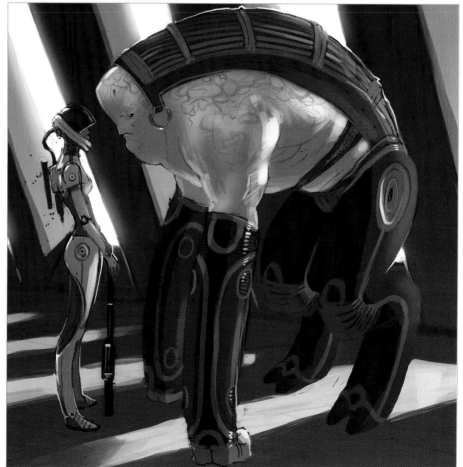

GETH

In the first story drafts, Saren's geth army was actually a bat-like species. But as Mass Effect's underlying theme of organics vs. machines emerged, the geth were rewritten as a synthetic lifeform.

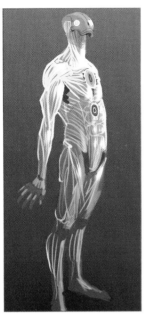

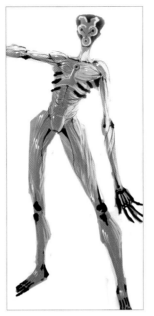

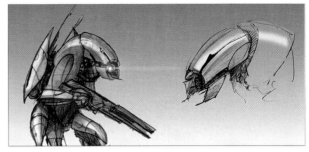

GETH

In contrast to the image of the classic metallic robot, the geth were designed to have a more lithe and sinewy appearance. One image (top left) appropriately captured this disconcerting approach, using rubbery tubing in place of veins and muscle striations.

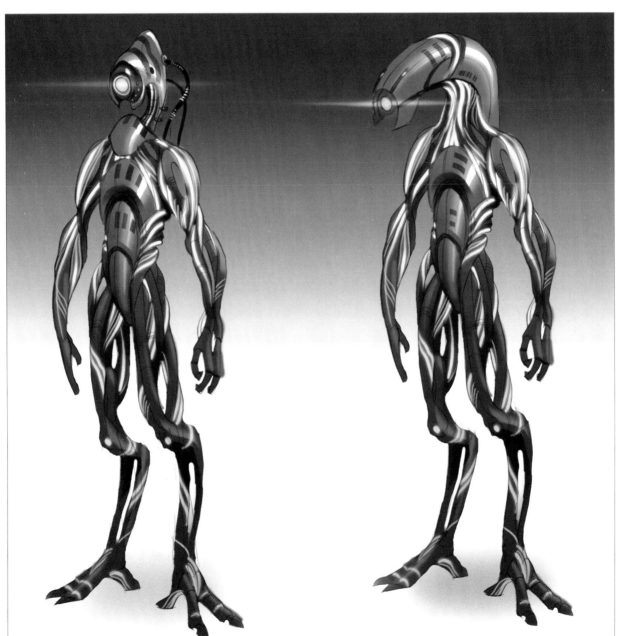

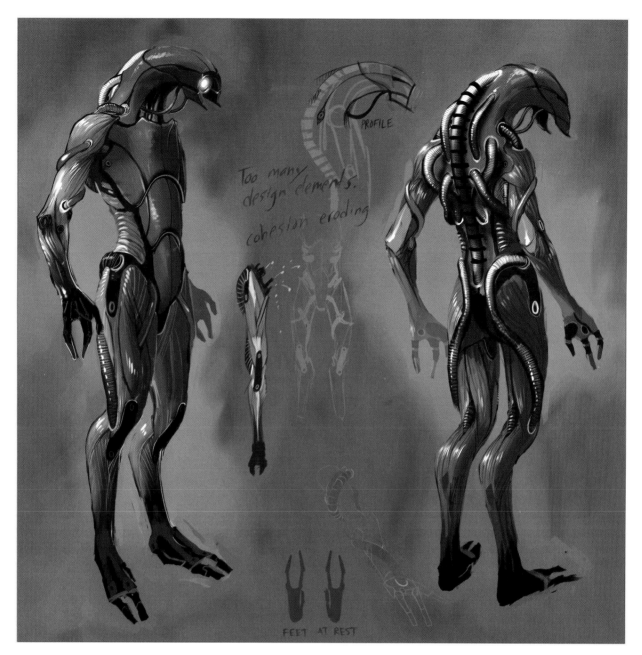

Too many
design elements,
cohesion eroding

PROFILE

FEET AT REST

GETH

Closing in on the final
design, detailed paintings
were made to establish
material properties and
other details that would
help the 3-D artists create
the geth, including the
single blue "eye" that casts
a horizontal lens flare.

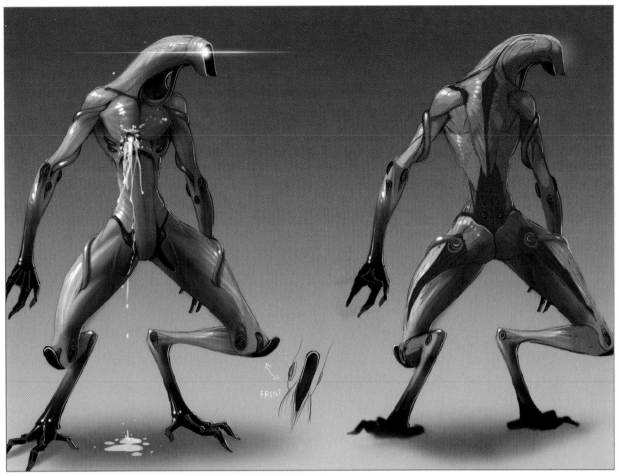

FRONT

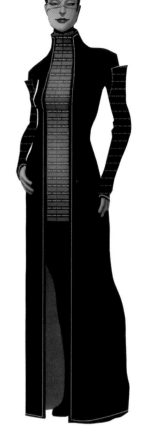

HUMAN CLOTHING

The design of human clothing helped establish the sleek and clean future of the Mass Effect universe. Early concepts focused on the graphical shapes and colors that would clearly differentiate characters from one another, such as mechanics, doctors, and bar patrons.

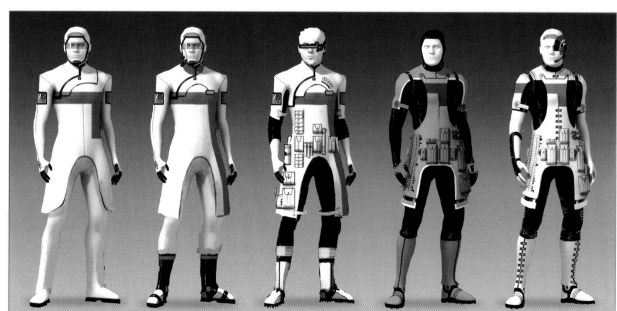

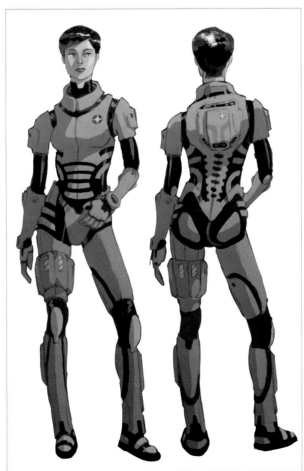

HUMAN ARMOR

To create a unique and consistent style, all armor designs would be based on the same principles: the use of straight lines and circular arcs to create strong geometric shapes.

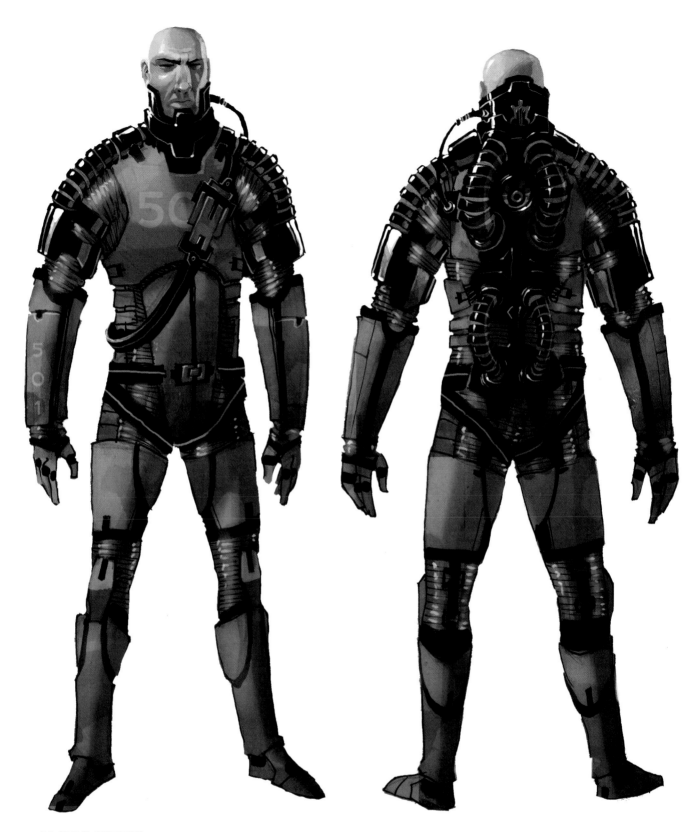

HUMAN ARMOR

The final design for standard human armor (opposite, in white) created a futuristic and form-fitting look while retaining a functional appearance that could be effective in combat. Other armors were required for unique characters, such as the hazmat suit (above and opposite, in red).

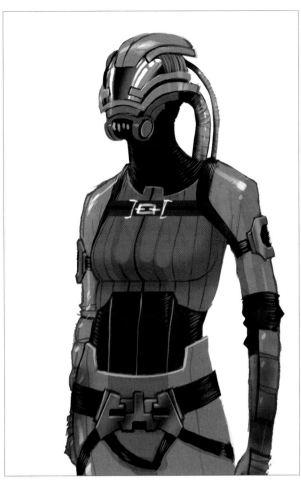

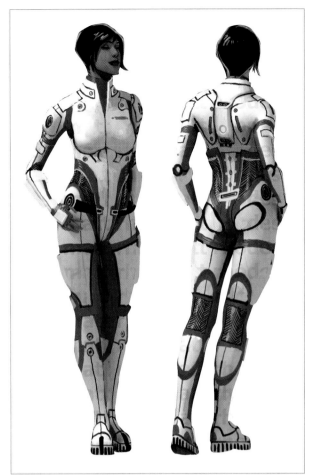

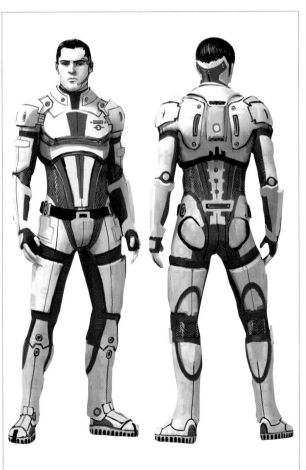

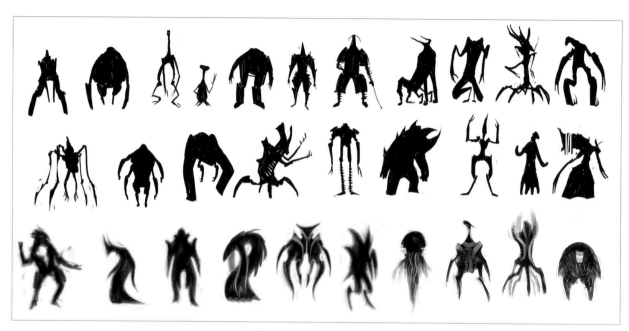

HANAR

To quickly evaluate a wide range of ideas for alien anatomies, small silhouette concepts were produced. Though some of the spider-like shapes were compelling, they were too similar to some of the other creatures, such as the rachni. Instead, the jellyfish concept (opposite) represented a unique direction for an exotic species. Later concepts developed the hanar into a more slender, lighter-than-air creature.

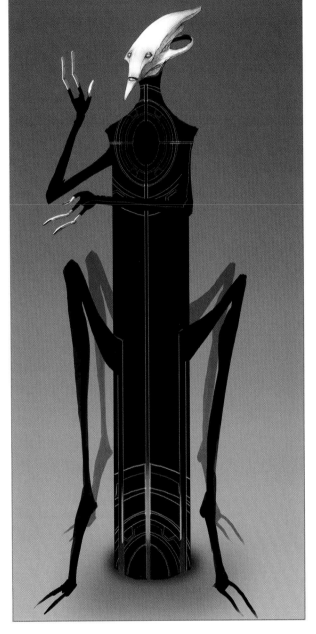

KROGAN

Filling the role of the big, brutish species in the Mass Effect universe, the krogan incorporated reptilian features. The final concept (opposite, top left) brought their design somewhat closer to human proportions, allowing them to move and fight as traditional soldiers.

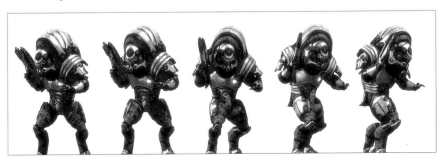

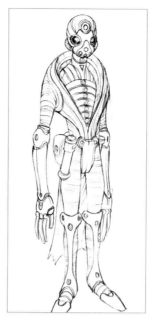

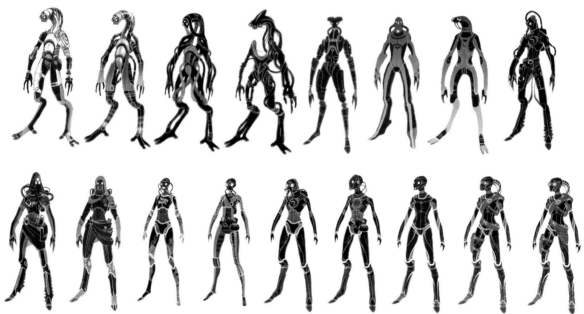

QUARIANS

Creators of the geth, the quarians were overrun by their creations and forced to leave their homeworld. Their visual similarity with geth anatomy helps connect their history. Quarian clothing, seemingly pieced together from scraps, was designed to reflect their nomadic nature.

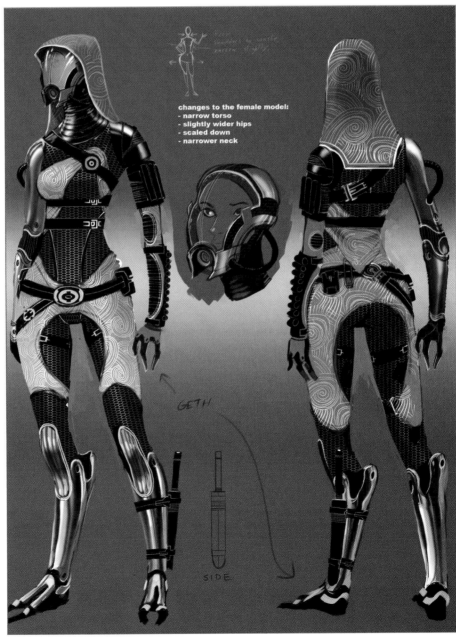

changes to the female model:
- narrow torso
- slightly wider hips
- scaled down
- narrower neck

GETH

SIDE

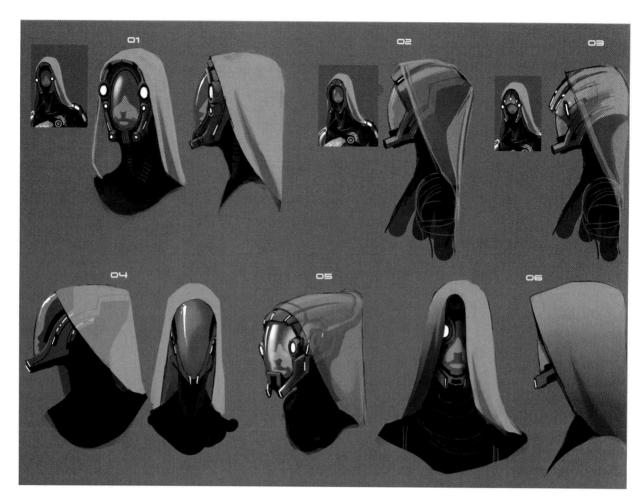

QUARIANS

Tali represents the appearance of only one member of her species. What others might look like—and what they might look like under their visors —remains a mystery.

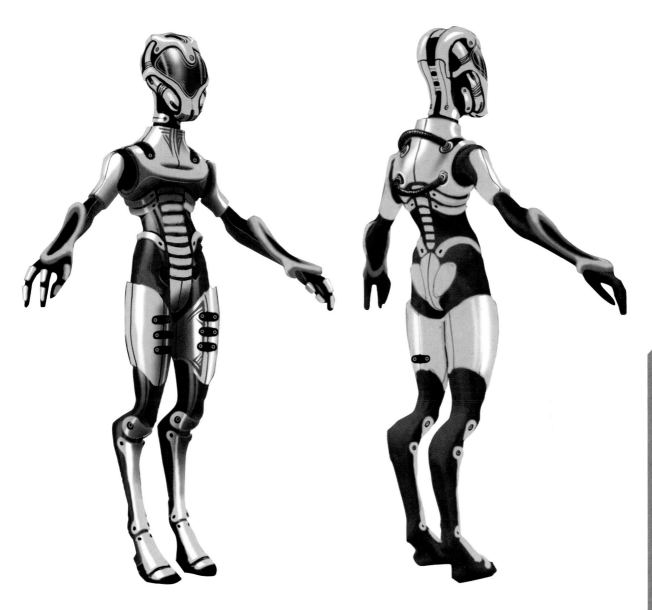

SALARIANS

To create a very alien and intellectual look, the salarians were inspired by the wide-eyed, delicate appearance of salamanders. Their bodies and armor were designed to support these qualities by creating a unique profile.

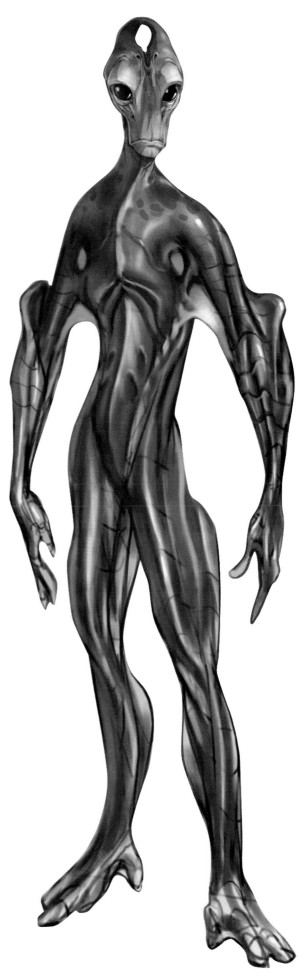

SALARIAN CLOTHING

For each species in Mass Effect, a range of clothing styles was required to create characters from various levels of society. The concept for the counselor robes (above) was approved as a final design, whereas many early concepts were never built (left).

SAREN

HAUNTED →

BLAH

SCARRED
AND PISSED

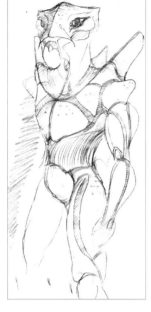

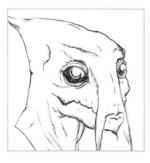

MIRRORED
ON CHEST

TURIAN GANG SYMBOL

REVERSE
MIRRORED
ON LEGS

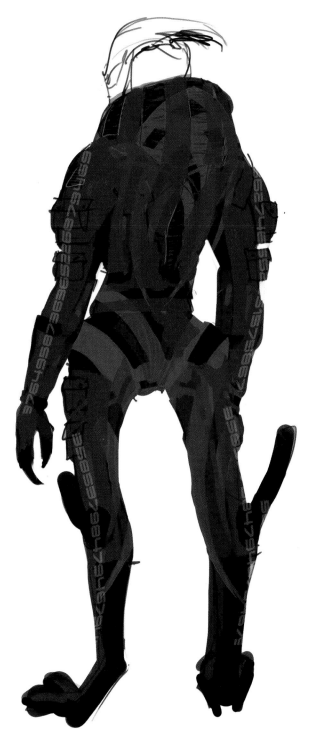

TURIAN

Knowing that Mass Effect's villain would be a turian, artists gave this species features that would support his intimidating character. The bony face plates give turian characters a stern, hawk-like appearance, while the wiry body frame implies a potential for stealthy movement.

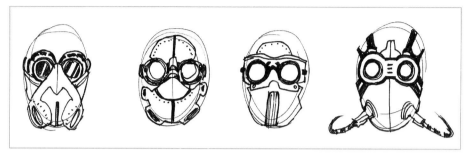

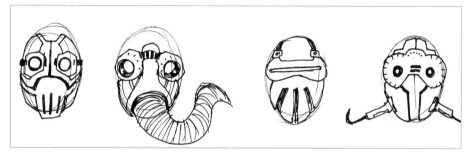

VOLUS

Sometimes a design seems to have a life of its own. The volus began as a heavily-clothed character with a gas mask (below) that developed into this lovable and portly final design (opposite). This final drawing inspired artists and writers to transform the volus into a diminutive, comical species.

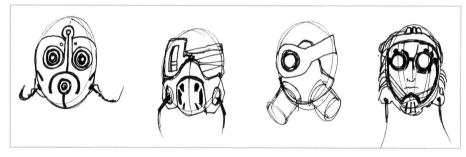

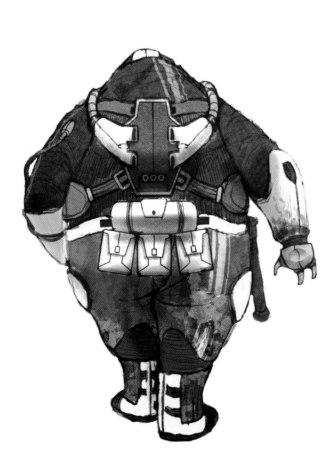

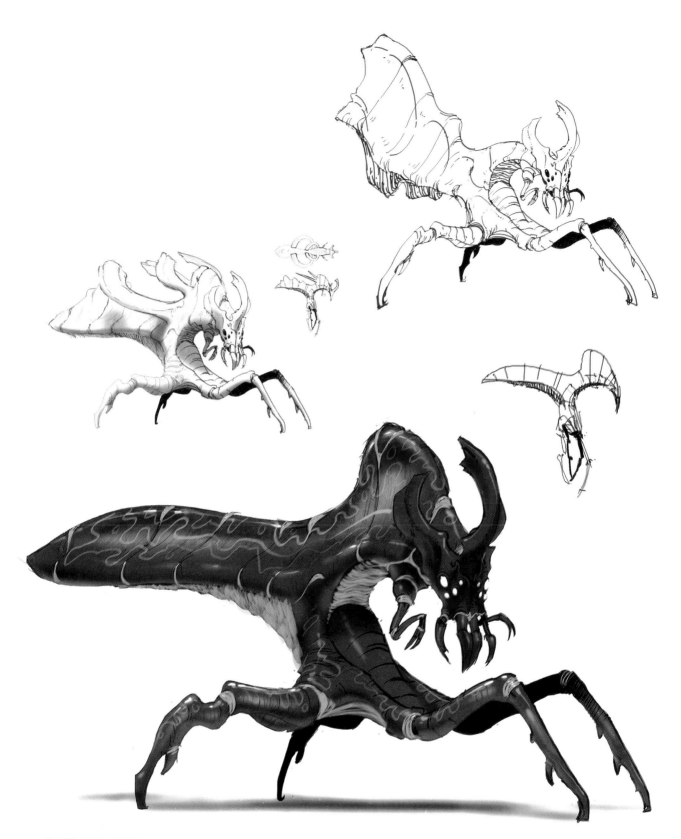

RACHNI QUEEN

While the rachni would initially appear as mindless monsters, the rachni queen would be surprisingly intellectual, in addition to being physically intimidating. Though she would be nearly 50 feet long, her design was inspired by tiny beetles and insects.

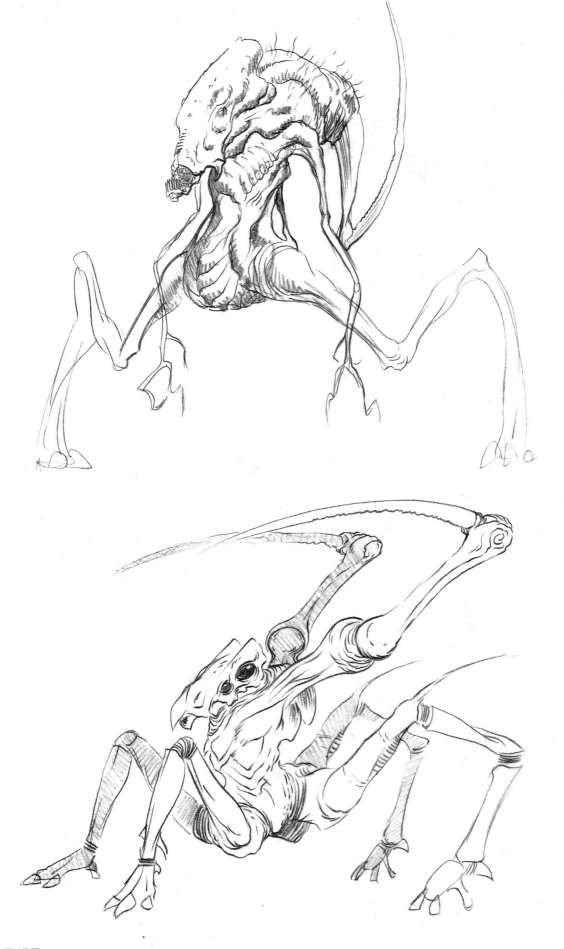

RACHNI

Early versions of the rachni showed a spider-like form with deadly pointed arms that could attack with a stabbing motion. These would later become whip-like appendages that could attack from a greater distance.

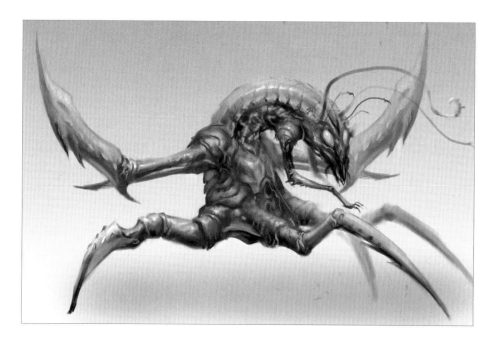

RACHNI

As the final design of the rachni took shape, ideas for rachni eggs and hive entrances were developed to provide locations for rachni to emerge from.

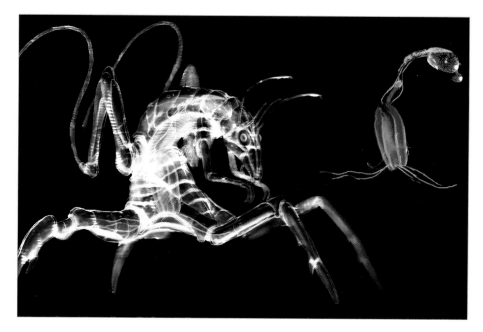

top down

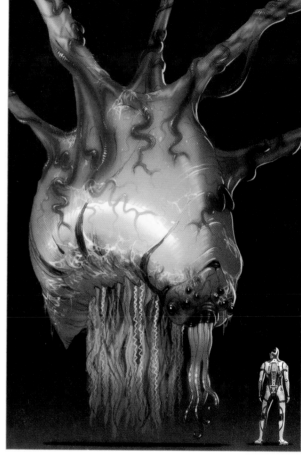

THE THORIAN

Although the Thorian was originally written as a plant-like creature, its design transformed into a more slug-like appearance, achieving a grotesque and intimidating form.

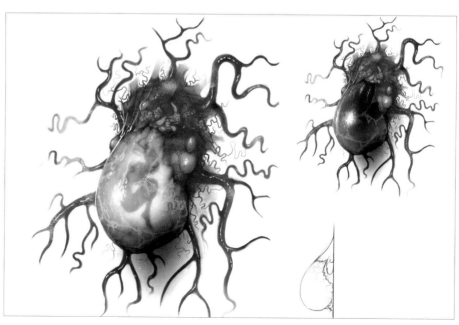

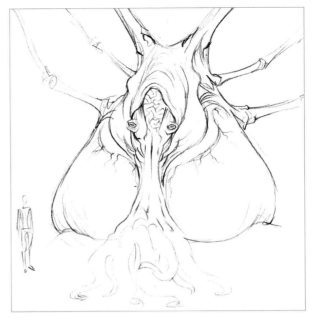

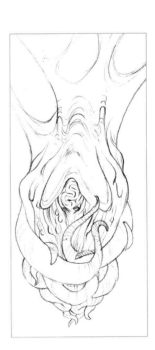

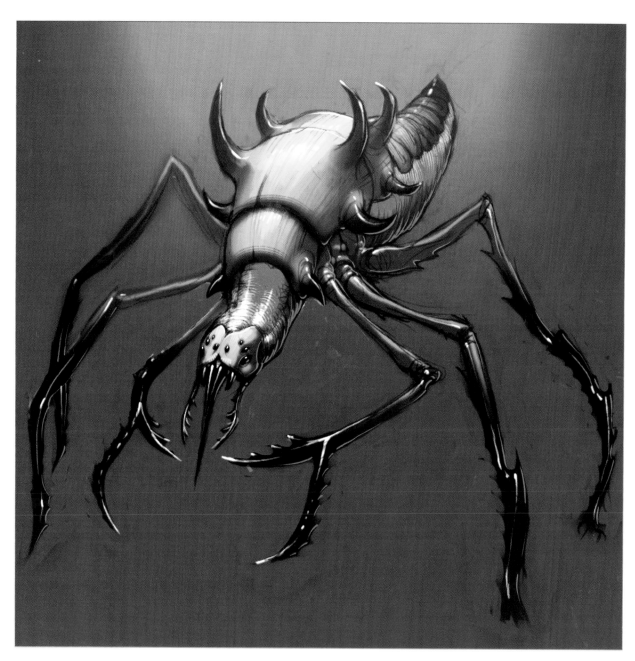

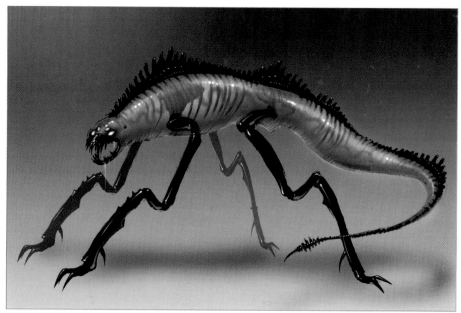

HARVESTERS

The harvester was meant to be a very large creature that could only be defeated with the use of the Mako all-terrain combat vehicle. Although its final design (opposite, center) was built, it was never used.

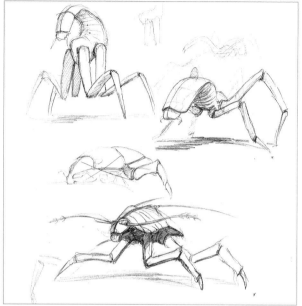

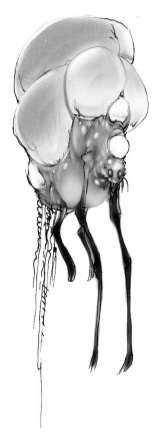

AMBIENT CREATURES

The Mass Effect universe is populated with a number of ambient creatures that give life to the environments. Gas bags (above, right) are lighter-than-air creatures that release poisonous fumes when "popped." Man-sized beetles (above, left) represent no danger but nonetheless, are a remarkable sight.

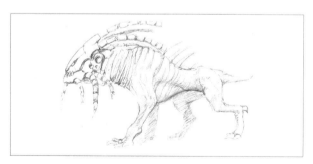

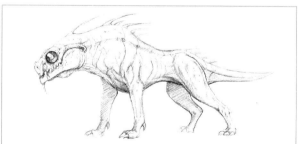

VARREN

Creature designs in the Mass Effect universe employ a simple device to make them seem alien: an unnatural combination of familiar earth creatures. The varren are a perfect example of this, combining the body of a dog with the scaly skin and bulbous eyes of a deep-sea fish.

THRESHER MAW

Possibly the largest creature in the Mass Effect universe, the thresher is able to burst from the soil without warning.

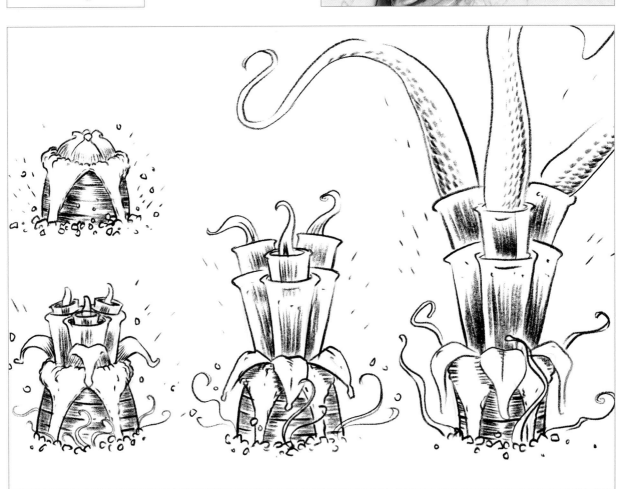

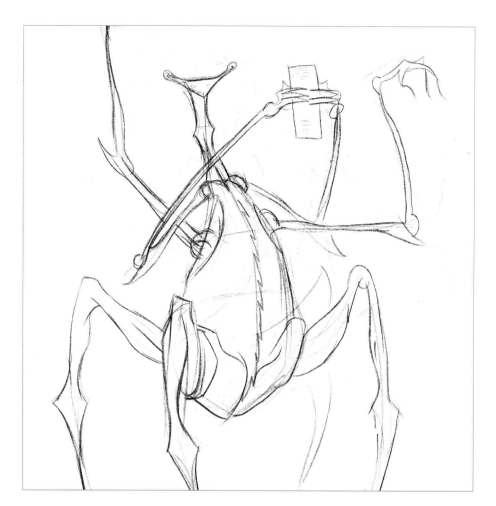

KEEPERS

To achieve the appearance of a "gentle insect", the design of the keepers was based on the praying mantis, with whimsical details (a vest and tiny backpack) to make them seem sentient.

x

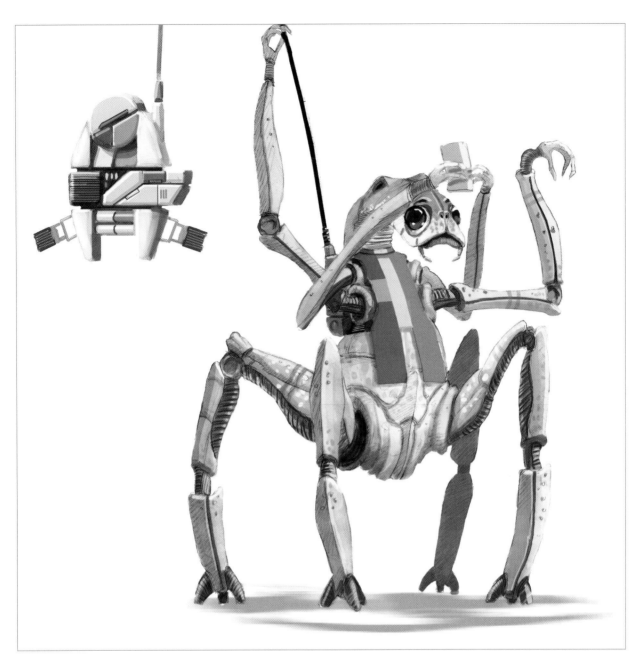

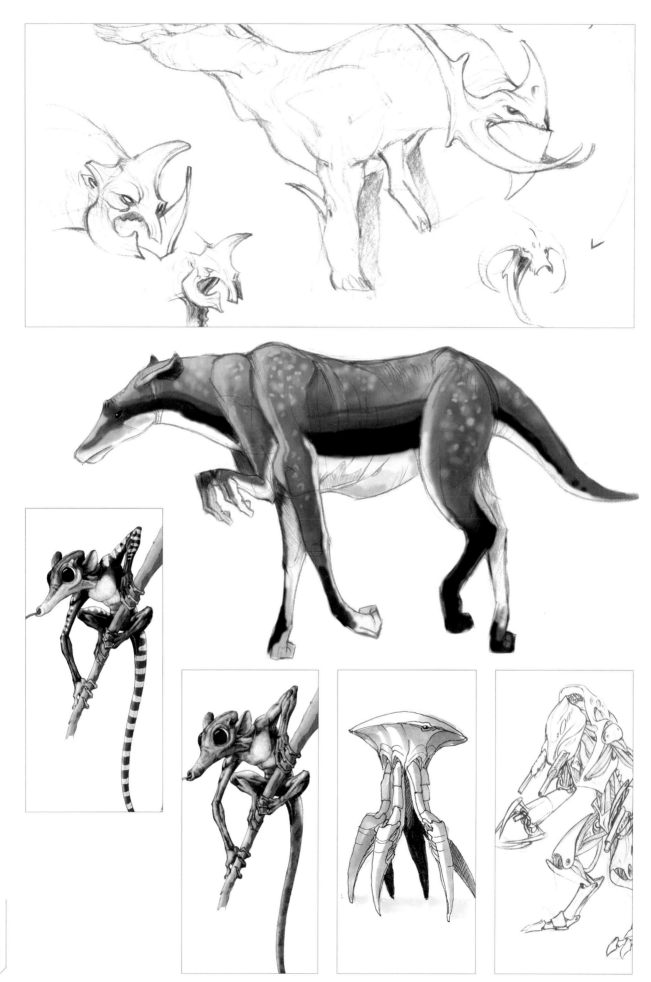

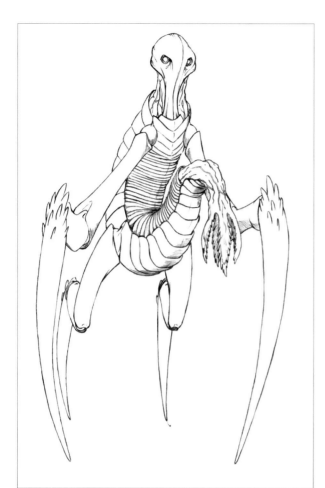

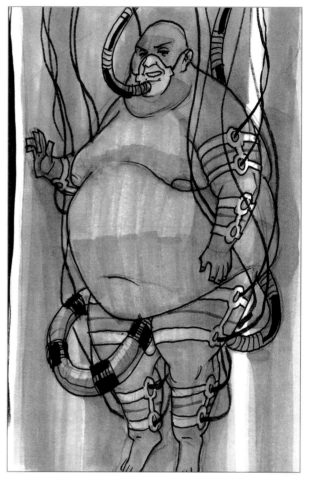

ADDITIONAL CONCEPTS

In the process of exploring ideas for creatures seen in Mass Effect, many excellent concepts were drawn but not built. A team favorite was the "space goat" (top, right).

TRANSPORT

How would interstellar space travel actually work? This is one of the first questions that need to must be answered—at least in fictional terms—when creating a futuristic setting. The rules that govern space travel will determine where you can go, how long it takes, and ultimately, what kinds of stories can be told. In Mass Effect, a system of enormous antennae called mass relays allows ships to travel hundreds of light-years in a matter of moments. Though these gigantic relays were left behind by an ancient civilization, the ships that use them belong to a variety of fleets—including the Human Alliance. This created opportunities for artists to not only design an armada of starships, but to also give each fleet a unique visual style. The most important ship of them all, however, would be Commander Shepard's: the SSV Normandy. It would not only serve as an environment for players to explore and a backdrop for some of Mass Effect's most dramatic moments, but it would almost need to be a character unto itself, playing the starring role in the game's most spectacular space battles.

03

THE MAKO

One early painting illustrated the adventurous spirit of exploring Uncharted Worlds in Mass Effect (above). It kicked off the formal design process for the Mako, the player's all-terrain combat vehicle. Knowing that players would have to traverse extremely rough terrain, the Mako needed large wheels and lots of ground clearance, while still having a sporty and futuristic look.

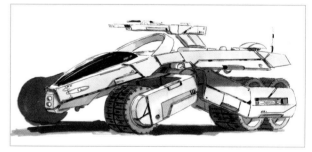

THE MAKO

Many different designs were considered, including floating vehicles (opposite). Some of these concepts were actually built and tested to evaluate their capability in traversing rugged terrain. The vehicle from the concept shown above can be seen in Mass Effect as a stationary vehicle and was once the front-runner for the Mako design.

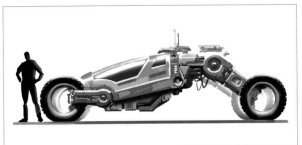

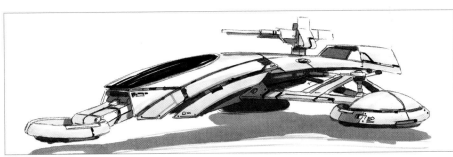

THE MAKO

The final concept for the Mako looked surprisingly sleek and futuristic for a vehicle with tremendous off-road ability. This resulted mainly from its wide wheelbase, and the pointed nose resembling the shark for which it is named.

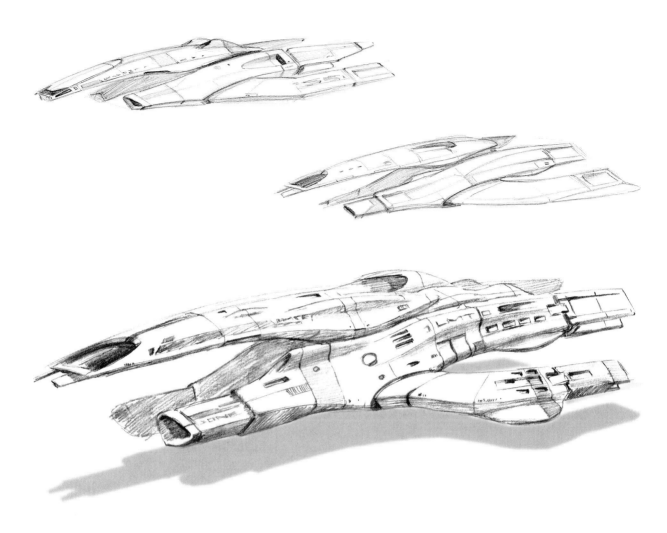

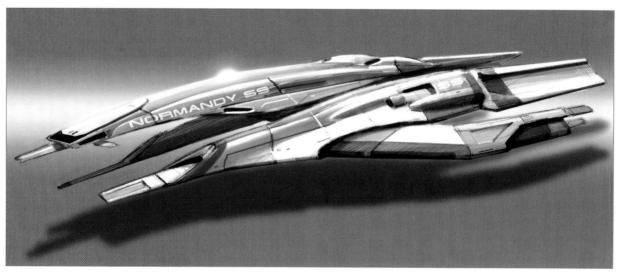

NORMANDY EXTERIOR

As the most advanced ship in the Human Alliance, the Normandy needed to look fast and stealthy. Early designs were inspired by the canted intakes and swept wings of the F-14 Tomcat fighter jet.

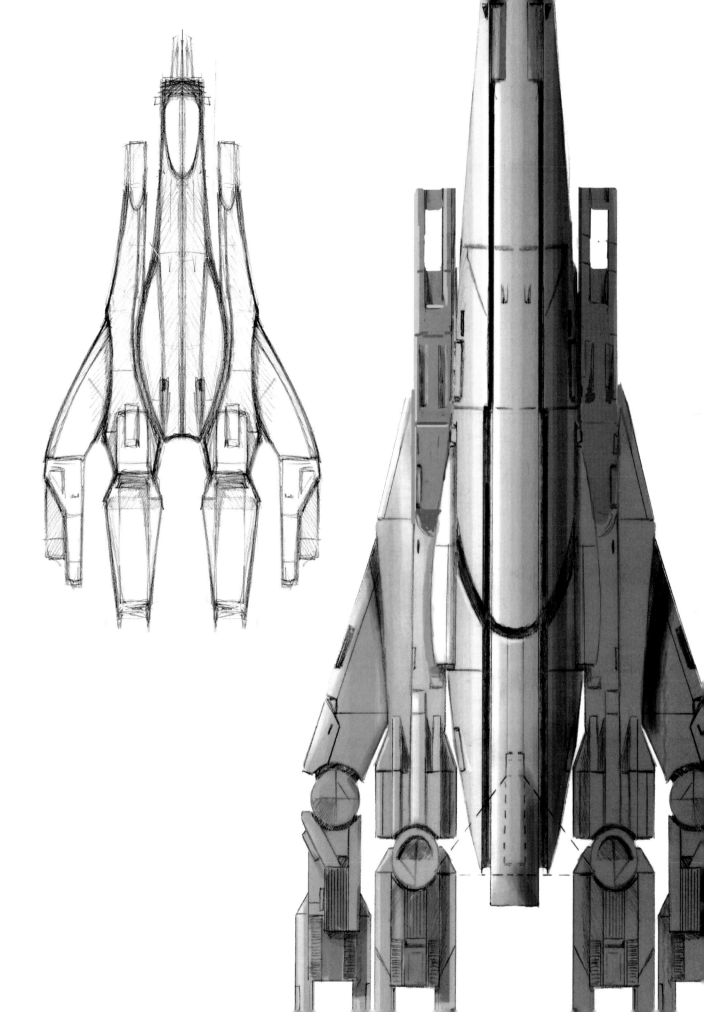

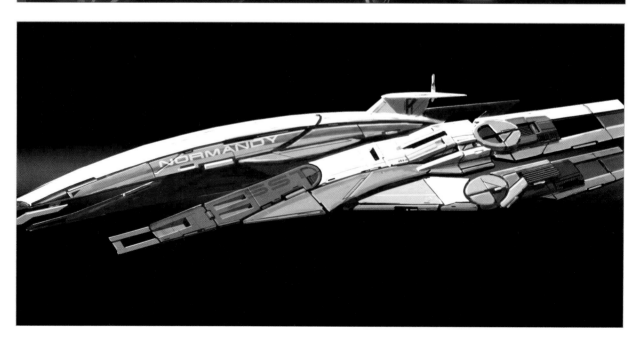

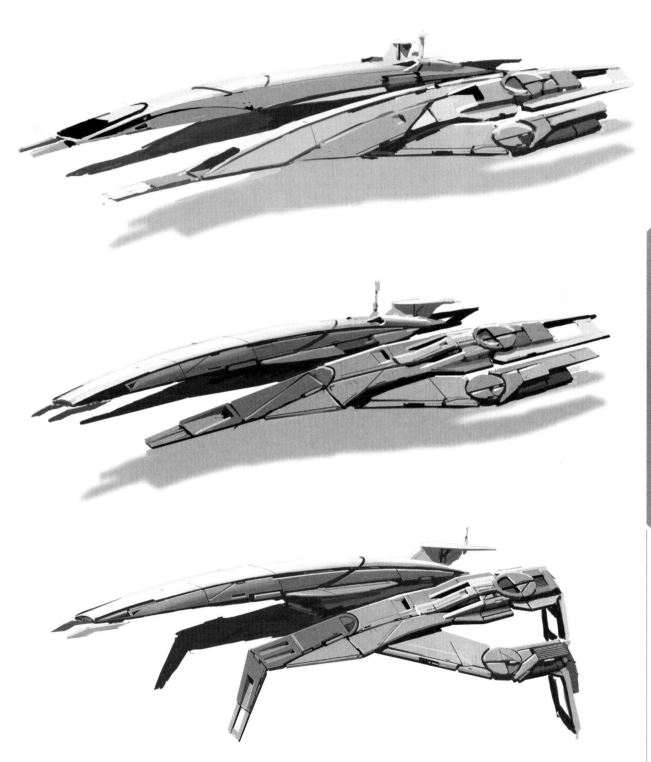

NORMANDY EXTERIOR
As the design was finalized, it was elongated even further to create a shape that looked capable of light-speed travel. But to ensure that it could come to a complete stop at a spaceport, vectored engine nozzles were added that also made it look more interesting when maneuvering.

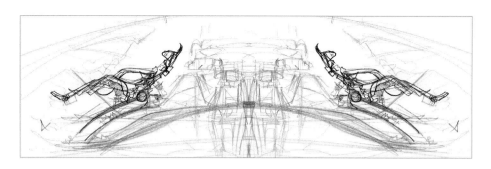

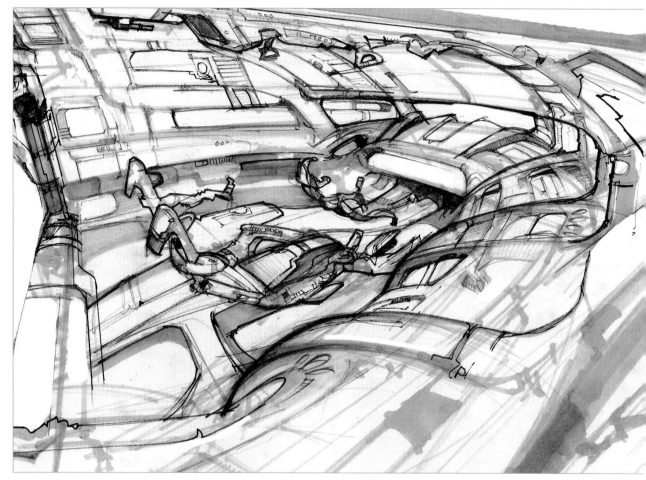

NORMANDY COCKPIT

The interior of the Normandy was meant to capture the purposeful, military atmosphere of a modern submarine. Crew would be seen working at bright computer screens in an otherwise dark environment. The cockpit would showcase this treatment as well as feature a narrow window to the world outside.

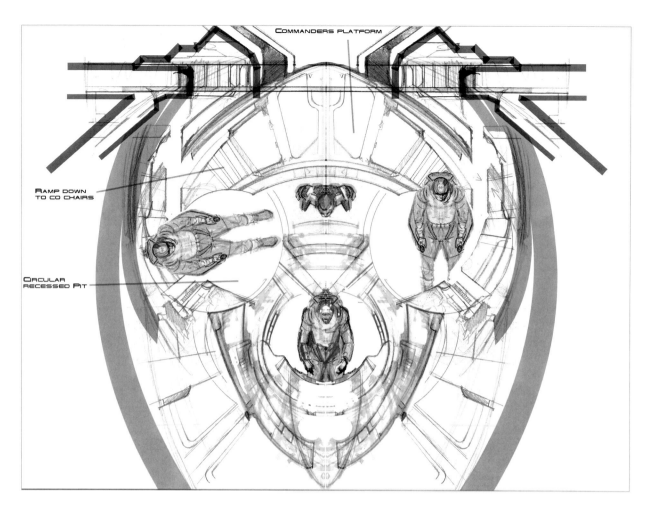

COMMANDERS PLATFORM

RAMP DOWN
TO CO CHAIRS

CIRCULAR
RECESSED PIT

NORMANDY INTERIOR

Several different approaches came together to visualize the Normandy's interior, such as marker renderings (above), rough 3-D models (opposite, top), and schematics (right).

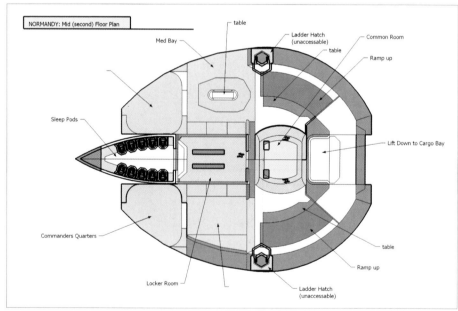

NORMANDY: Mid (second) Floor Plan

Med Bay

table

Ladder Hatch (unaccessable)

Common Room

table

Ramp up

Sleep Pods

Lift Down to Cargo Bay

Commanders Quarters

table

Ramp up

Locker Room

Ladder Hatch (unaccessable)

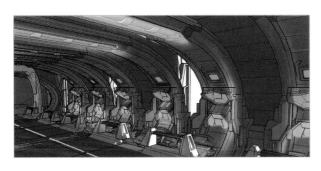

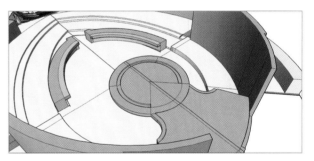

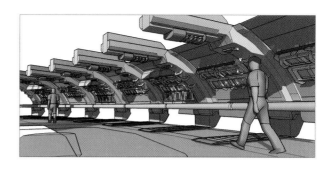

NORMANDY MID-DECK

The complex environment of a starship interior made it essential to draw upon 3-D sketching software to visualize such locations as the galley and sleep pod areas.

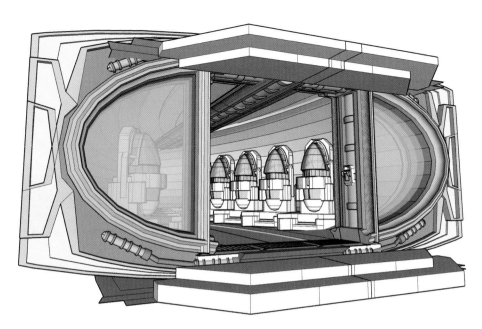

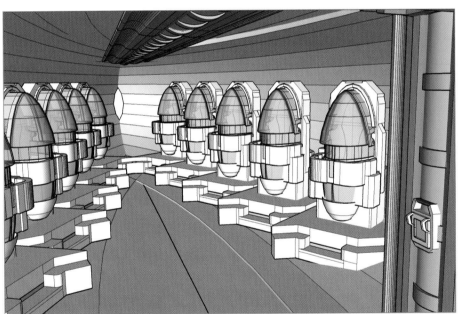

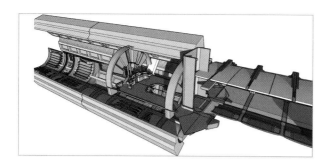

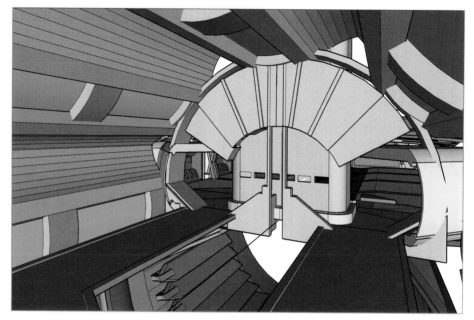

NORMANDY ENGINE ROOM

Though this area was relatively straightforward in visual terms, the enormous power of the engine was brought to life with large moving parts, impressive electrical effects, and thundering engine sounds.

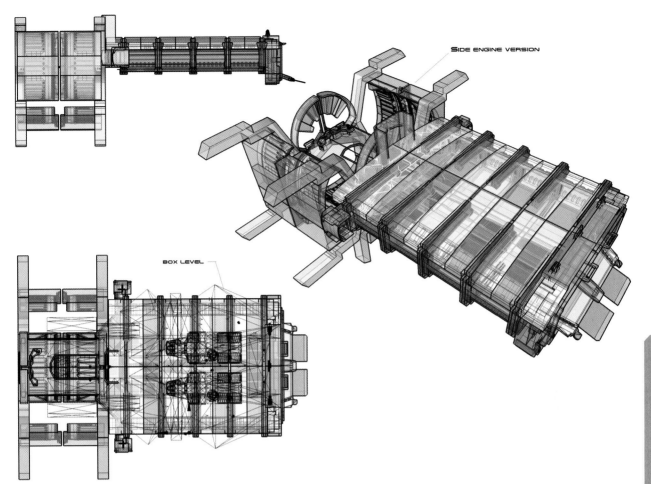

SIDE ENGINE VERSION

BOX LEVEL

NORMANDY CARGO BAY

Using pools of saturated color, the lighting of the cargo bay reinforces the claustrophobic feeling of being inside the belly of a starship.

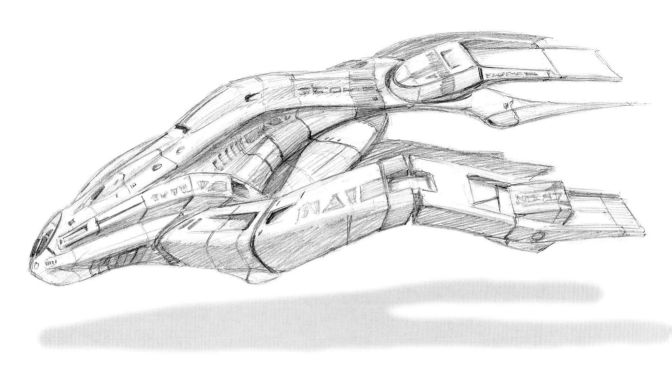

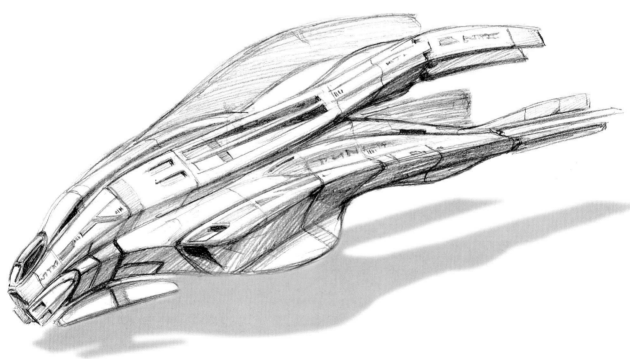

HUMAN SHIPS

Each species' starships was given a unique look. Ships of the human fleet incorporated highly organic shapes so that they seem to swim through space. Originally drawn as early designs for the Normandy, they later became possibilities for human cargo ships.

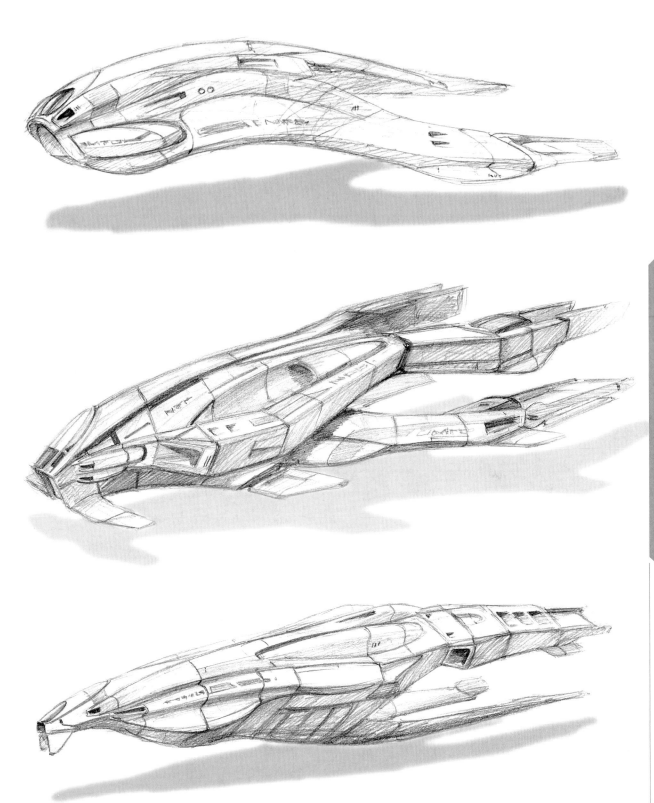

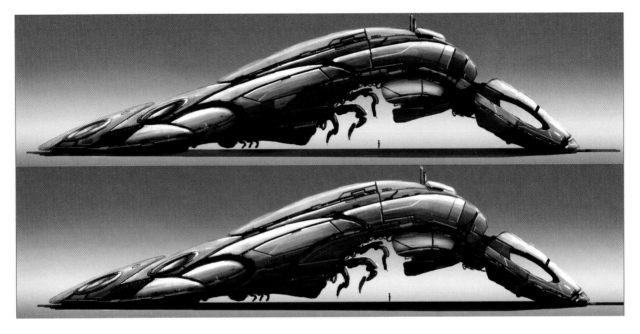

GETH SHIPS

To give them an intimidating appearance, geth ships were inspired by the tail-down posture a hornet takes when preparing to sting. Tiny "feelers" on the undersides of the ships enhance their insect-like profiles.

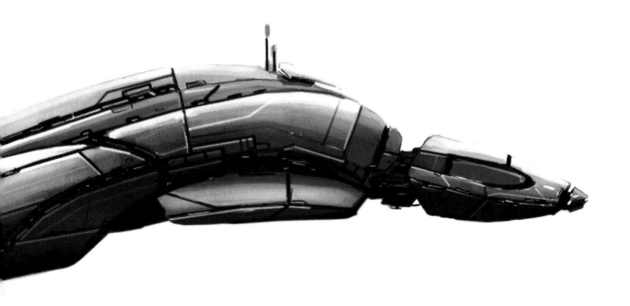

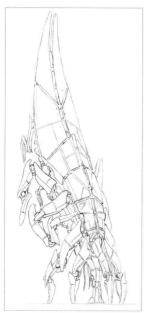

SOVEREIGN

Standing more than a mile tall, Sovereign is easily the largest ship in Mass Effect. To enhance its size, it was imagined that its presence and power would disrupt the weather (bottom, left). Features reminiscent of an insect's anatomy were added to further tie it to the geth and the other synthetic species in Mass Effect.

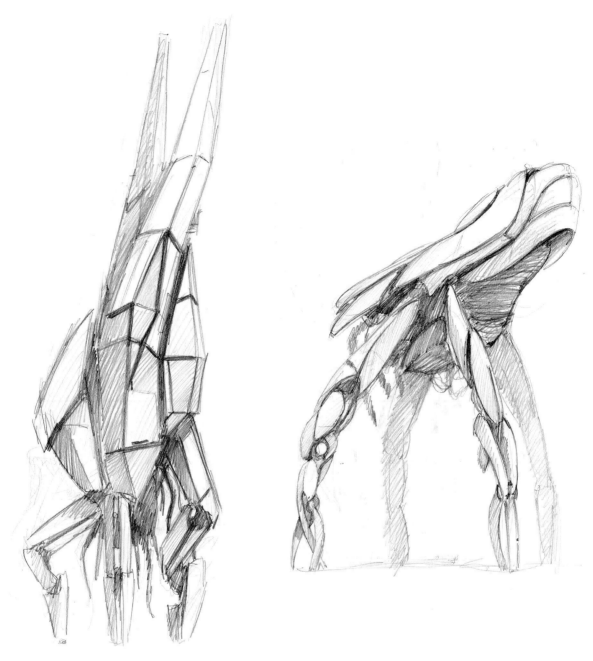

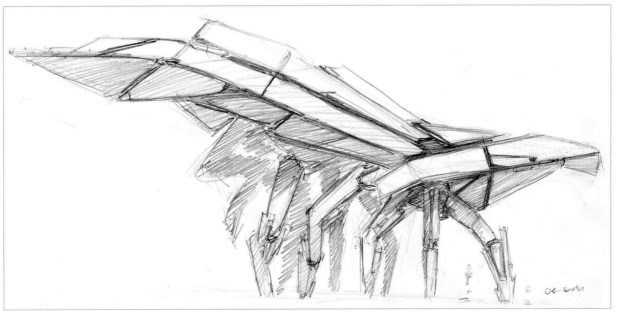

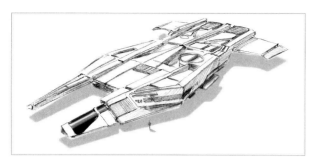
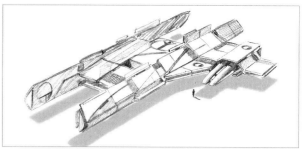
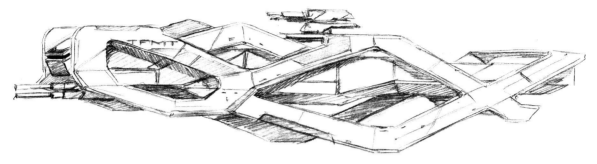
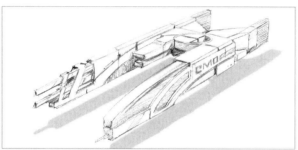
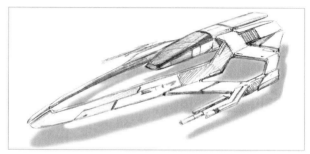
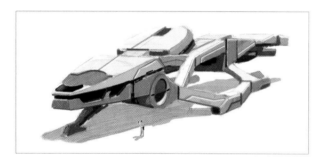

HUMAN SHIPS

These additional ship designs show some of the alternate ideas for the starship Normandy, as well as possibilities for cargo ships and fighters.

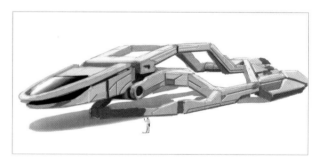
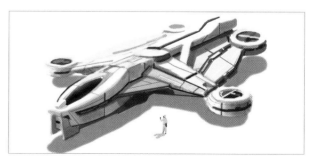

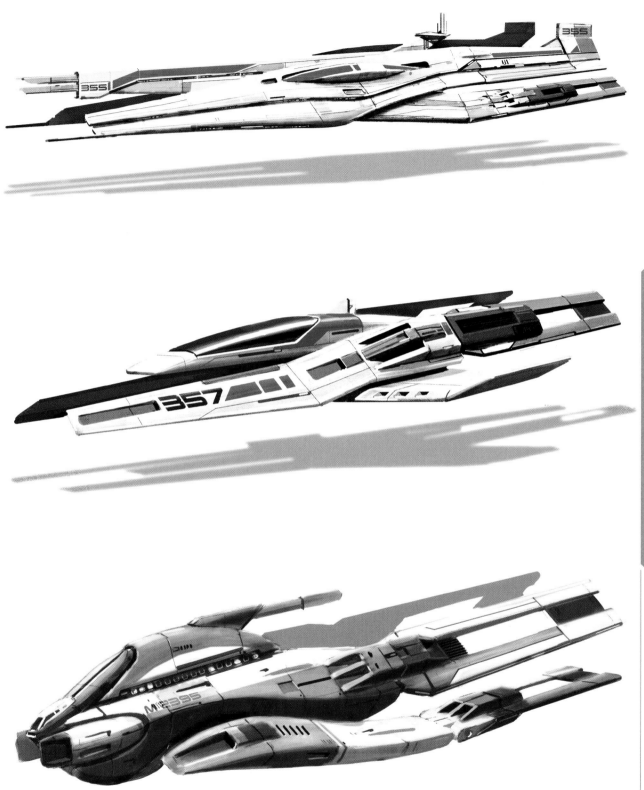

HUMAN SHIPS

Though these drawings are shown at the same size, they represent ideas for a huge destroyer (top), a one-man fighter (middle), and a heavy cruiser (bottom).

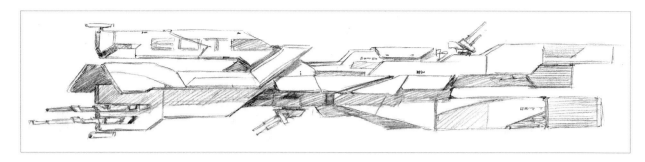

HUMAN SHIPS

At one point in the concepting process, human ships were heavily geometrical. These freighter designs incorporated harsh boxy lines and long circular arcs. Even the early fighter design (below) was primarily composed of straight lines.

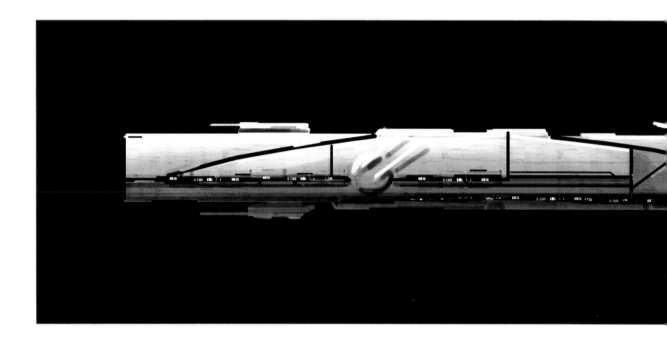

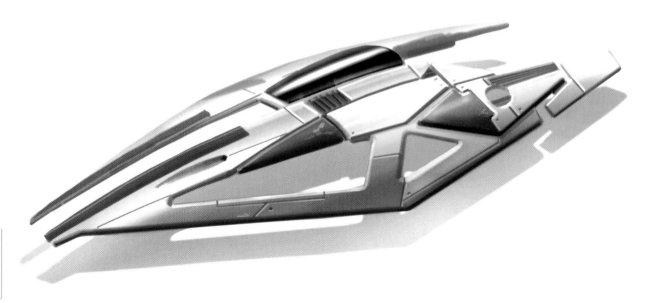

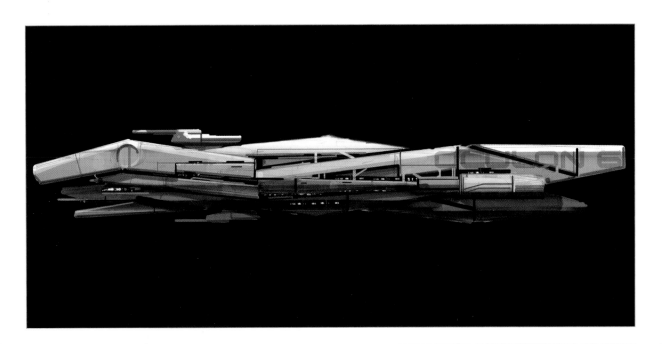

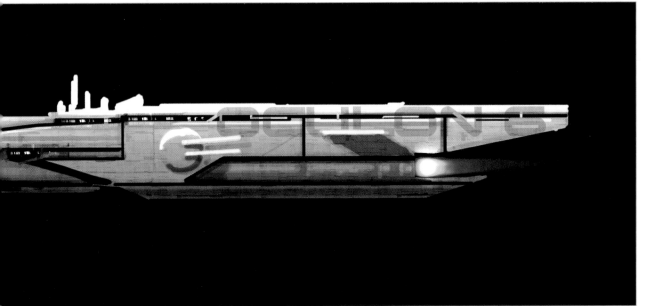

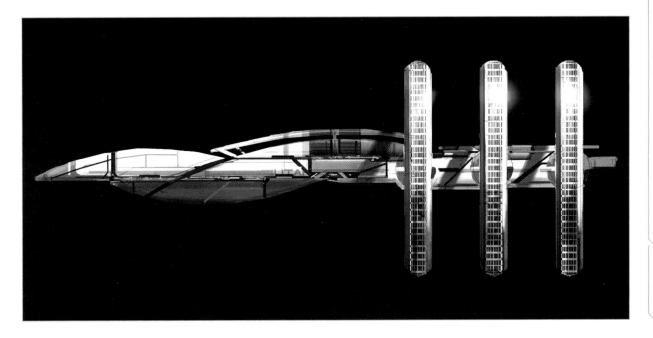

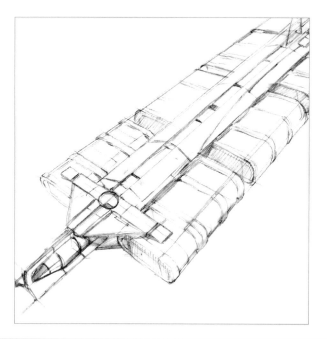
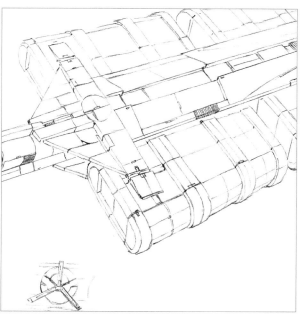
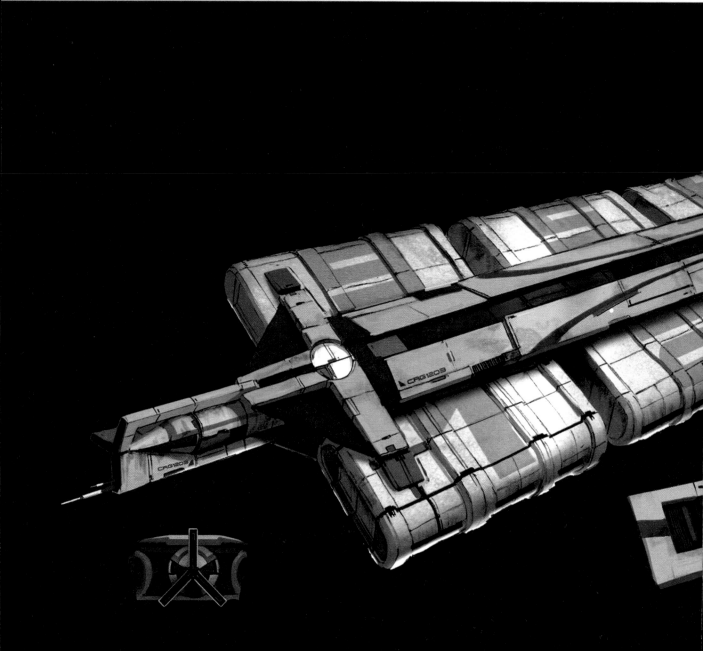

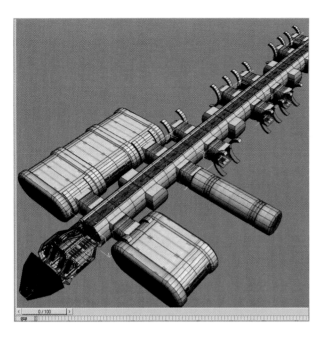

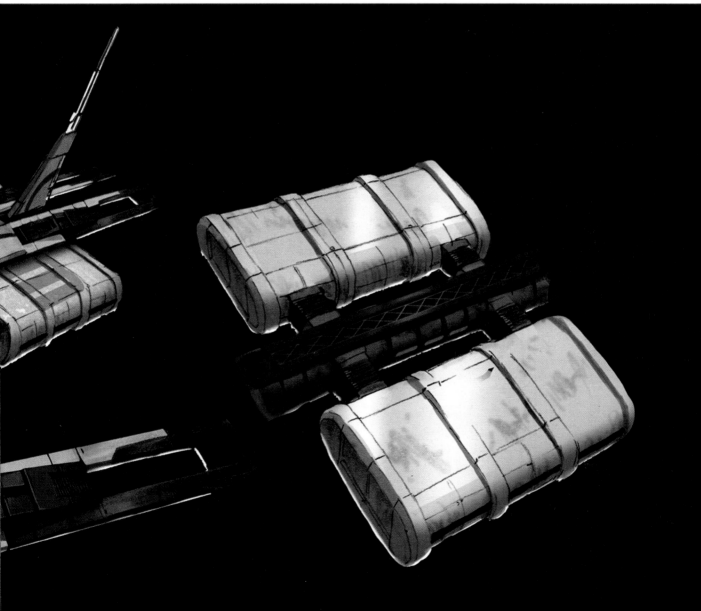

FREIGHTERS

These bare-bones cargo ships can be found throughout the galaxy. With a simple spine holding together a series of reusable containers, the designs are obviously based more on economy than performance or aesthetics.

TURIAN SHIPS

Turian ships incorporated layers of plates to roughly symbolize the feathered appearance of the turians themselves.

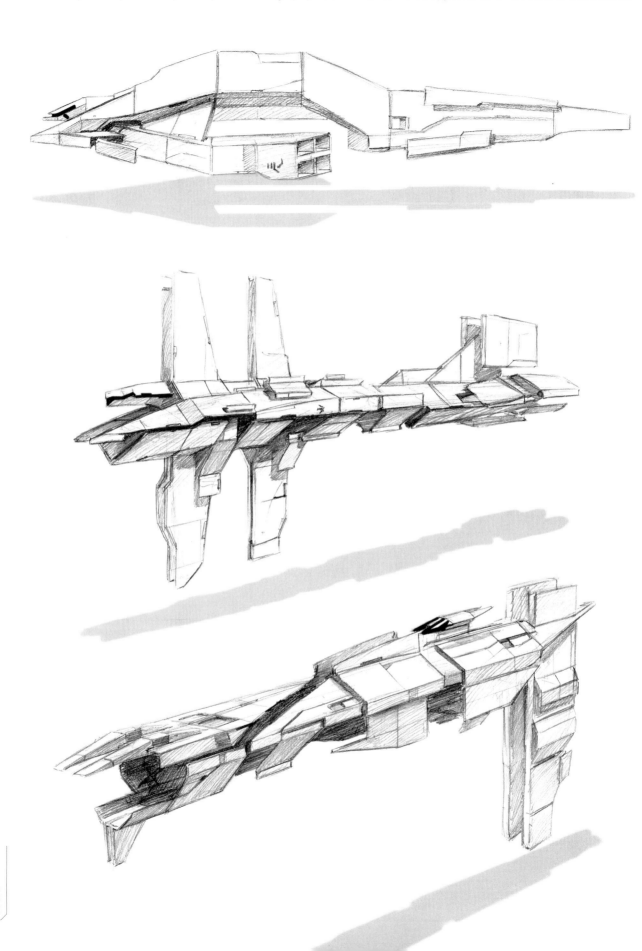

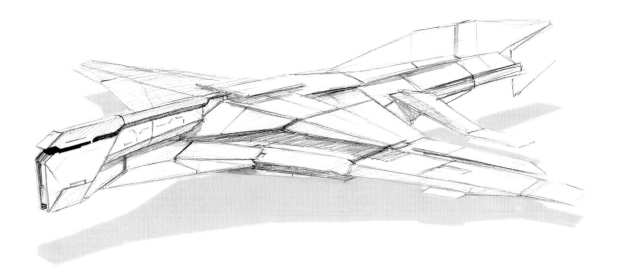

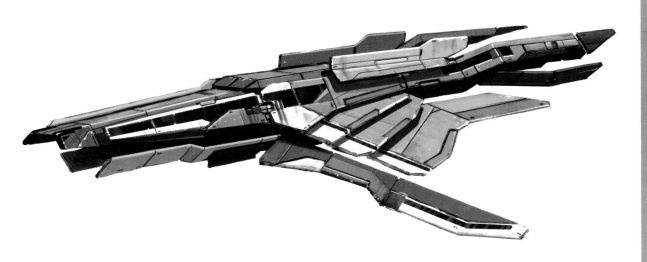

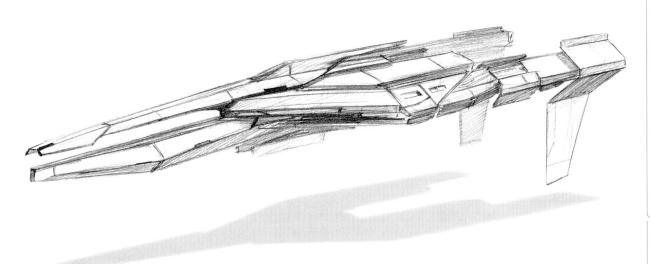

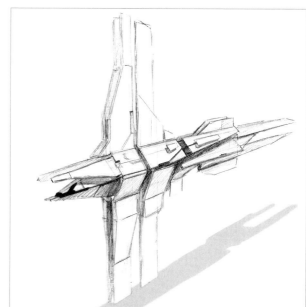

TURIAN SHIPS

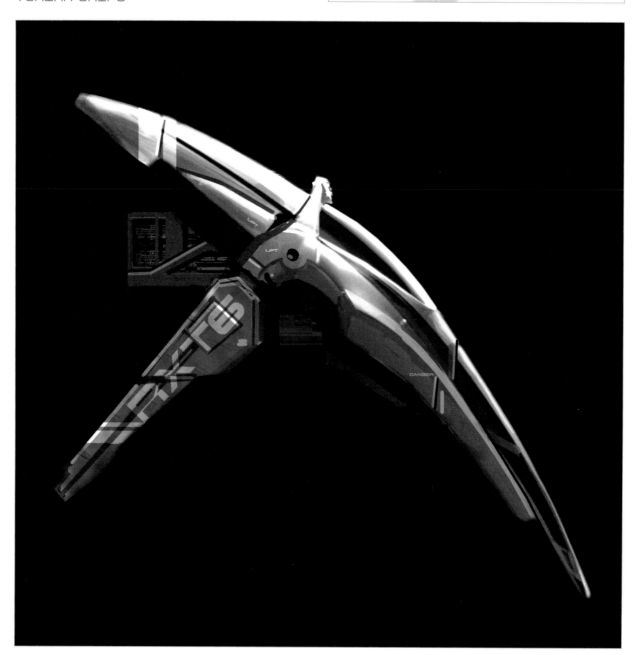

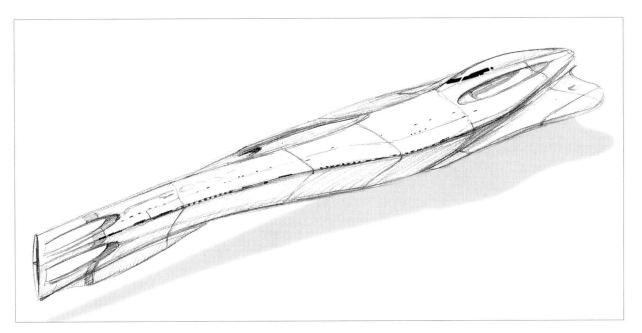

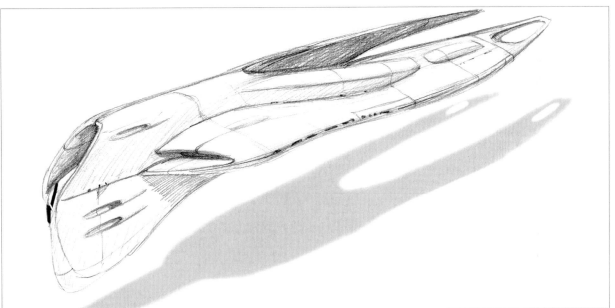

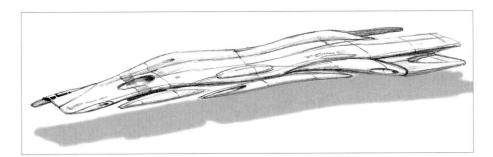

SALARIAN SHIPS

In a reference to the salarians' salamander-like appearance, the smooth, rounded appearance of the salarians ships makes them look as much like ocean-going vessels as starships.

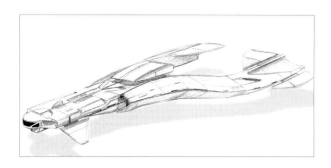

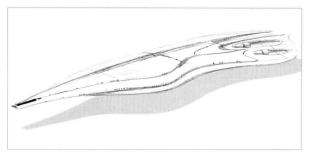

SALARIAN SHIPS

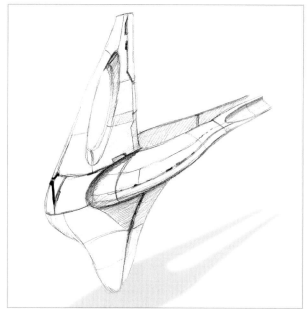

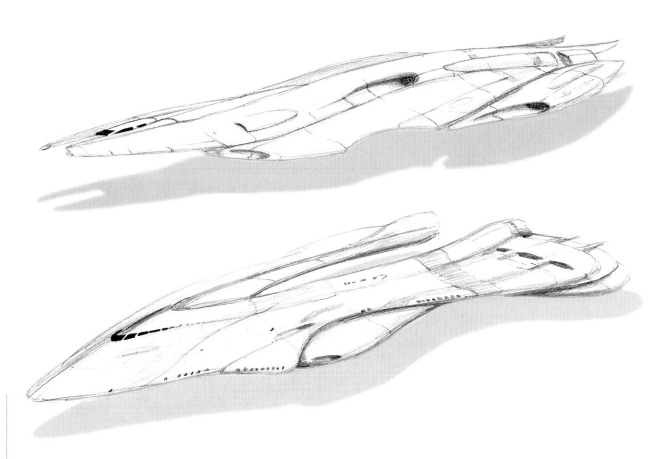

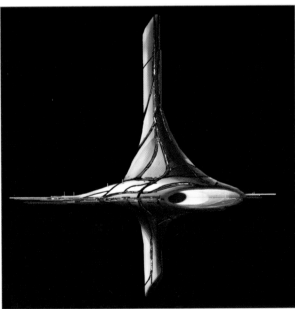

THE DESTINY'S ASCENSION
Built by the asari, the Ascension was one of the biggest starships in Mass Effect. But the Citadel and mass relays were large enough to make even ships of this size seem tiny.

A GALAXY OF DETAILS

Minute details might be the last thing one would think of in the production of an epic videogame, but artists must design and build countless small objects to complete the illusion of a functioning world. Some of these objects have an obvious appeal, such as the arsenal of futuristic weapons strapped to Commander Shepard's armor. Others, like beds and computer stations, simply provide context and functionality to each area in the game, while reinforcing Mass Effect's sleek and futuristic art style through their unique designs.

04

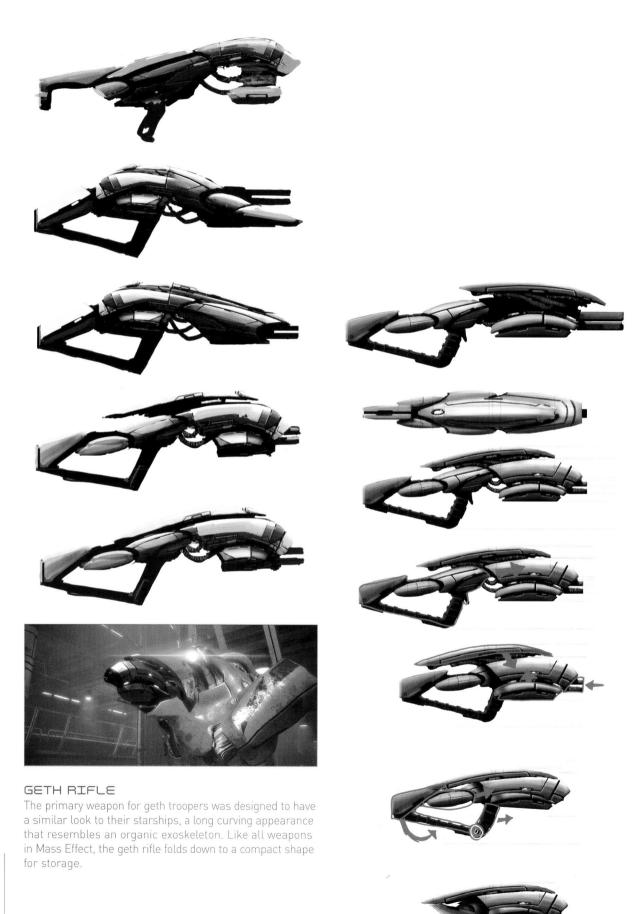

GETH RIFLE

The primary weapon for geth troopers was designed to have a similar look to their starships, a long curving appearance that resembles an organic exoskeleton. Like all weapons in Mass Effect, the geth rifle folds down to a compact shape for storage.

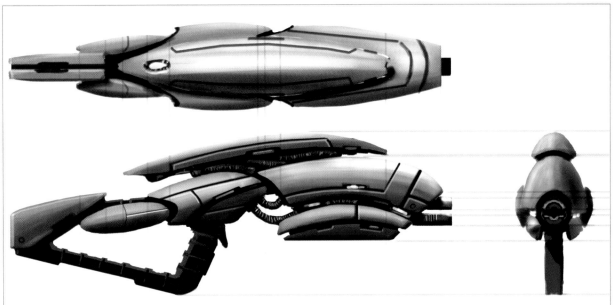

GETH DRONE

The drones were built and controlled by the geth, so they bear similar features—the single blue eye light and vaguely metallic surface.

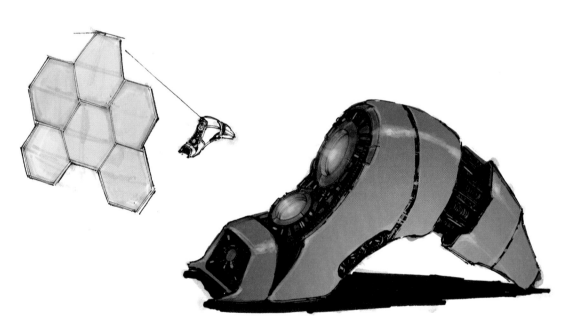

HEX BARRIERS

This concept shows how the hex barriers were originally meant to be projected from stationary objects. This was later simplified by having the geth create the barriers directly.

GETH HEAVY DRONE AND FLYER

The geth heavy drone (top) provided a fast-moving enemy, while the flyer (below) was
designed to give normal geth troopers a raised platform for attacking the player.
Ultimately, Saren would be the only character to use the flyer.

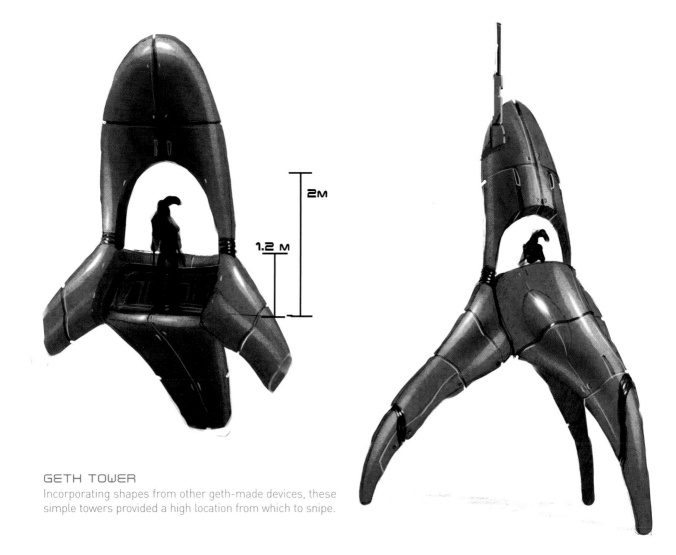

2M

1.2 M

GETH TOWER

Incorporating shapes from other geth-made devices, these
simple towers provided a high location from which to snipe.

GETH TURRET

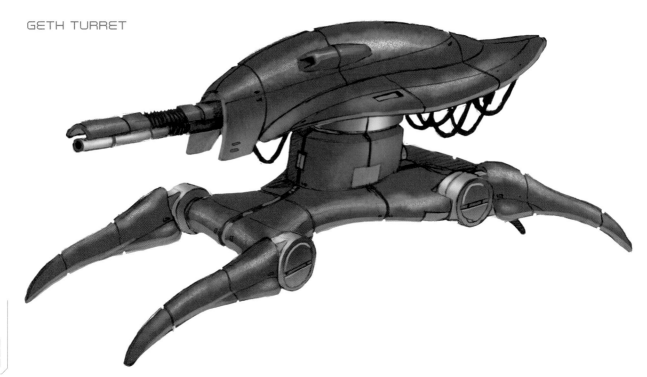

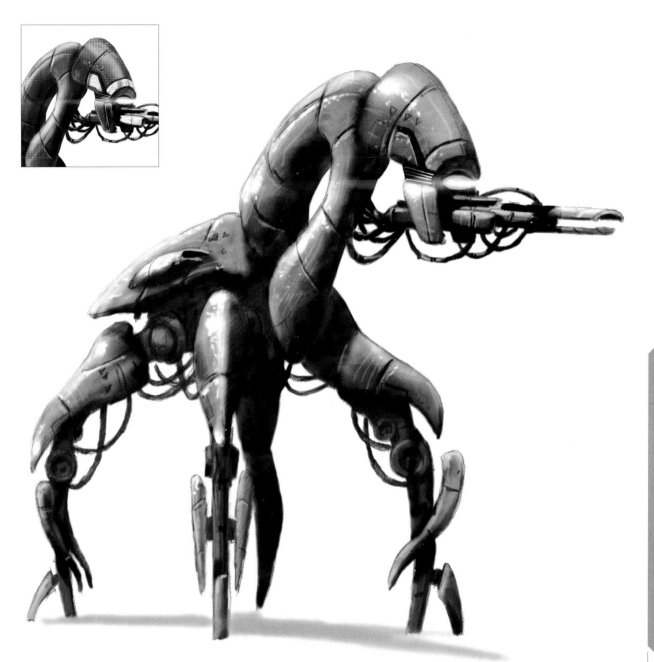

GETH ARMATURE

The geth have evolved into many distinct forms. To create the particularly large and dangerous enemies for Mass Effect, a four-legged giant was designed. The head-mounted turret was removed late in development to allow for omni-directional aiming.

ELECTRONIC EQUIPMENT

Mass Effect's design sense is particularly prominent in the equipment and appliances that detail the environment. Sweeping arcs meet straight lines to form elegant geometry that seems functional but futuristic.

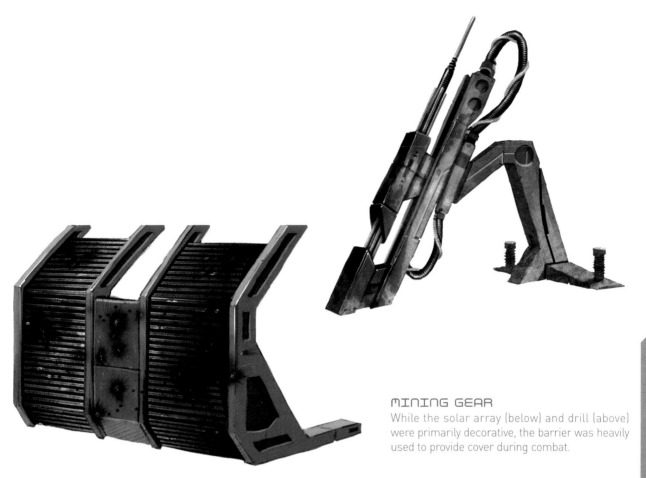

MINING GEAR

While the solar array (below) and drill (above) were primarily decorative, the barrier was heavily used to provide cover during combat.

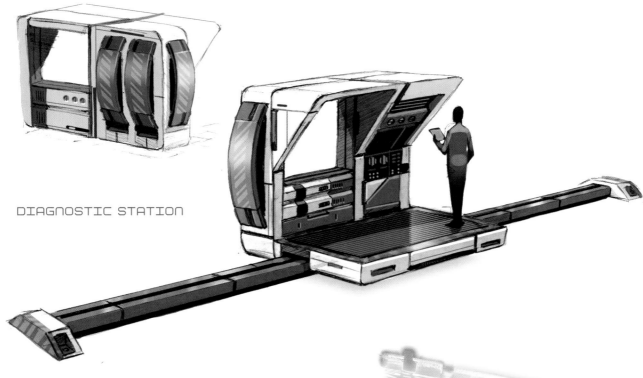

DIAGNOSTIC STATION

PLEASURE POD
The asari Consort makes use of these pods for privacy and comfort, but they were originally meant to hang from the ceilings of the Citadel's seedier establishments to showcase exotic dancers.

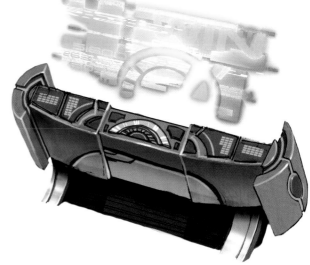

GAMING TABLES

TRANSMITTER TOWER

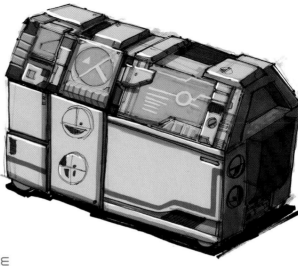

GENERIC APPLIANCE

Sometimes objects without an obvious purpose are required, so designers can place them in the environment for players to use as interactive objects or tactical cover during combat.

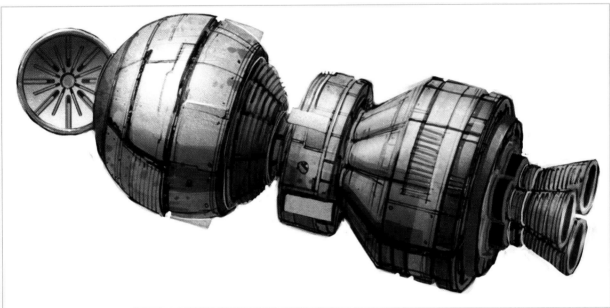

SPACE DEBRIS

Objects like the escape pod (middle) and the downed satellite (bottom) created opportunities for discovery and exploration on Uncharted Worlds.

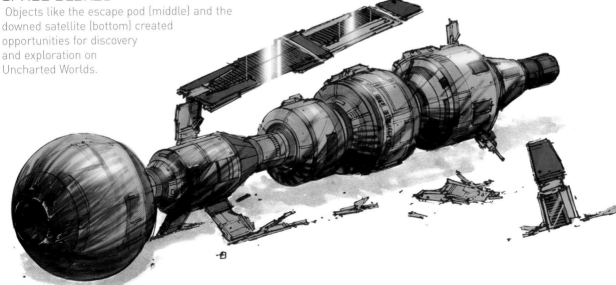

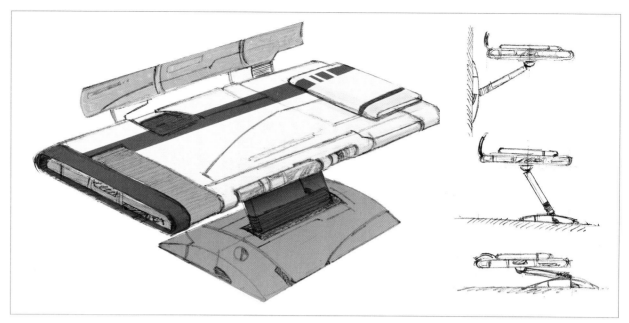

RETRACTABLE BED

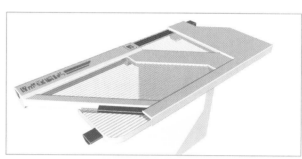

DESKS

WORKSTATION

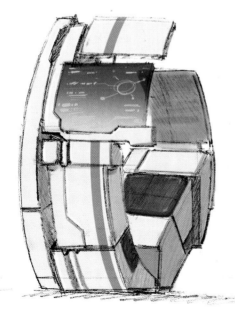

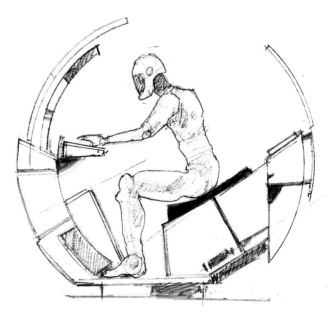

LOUNGE TABLE

DESK AND LAMP

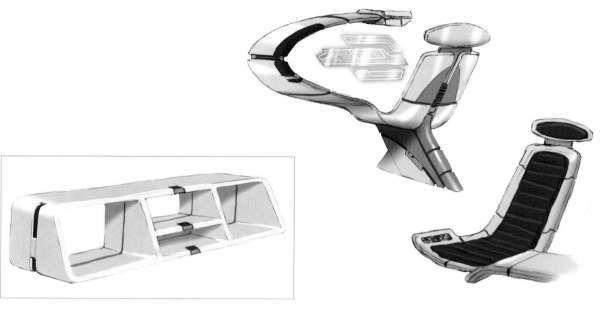

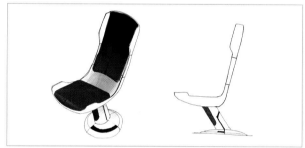

LIVING QUARTERS

Because players are free to explore a wide range of environments in Mass Effect, objects had to be built to detail everything from the exotic to the everyday. Even futuristic versions of desks, chairs, and shelves had to be made to flesh out the homes, offices, and living quarters of various characters.

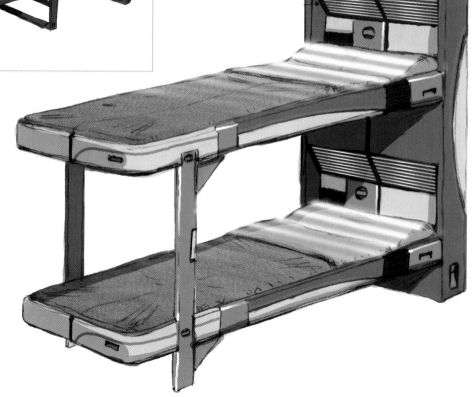

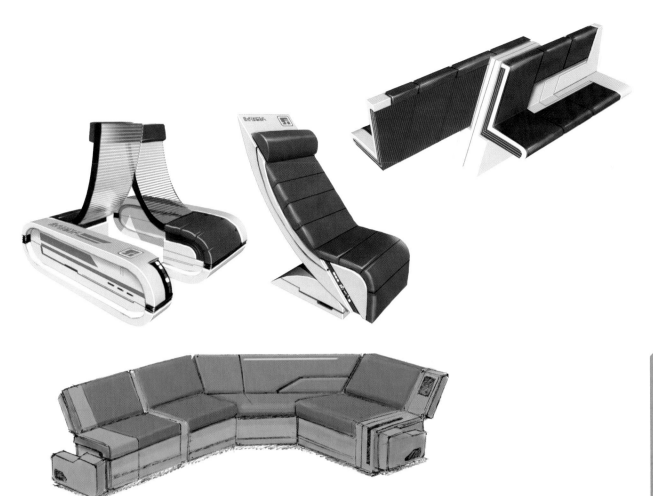

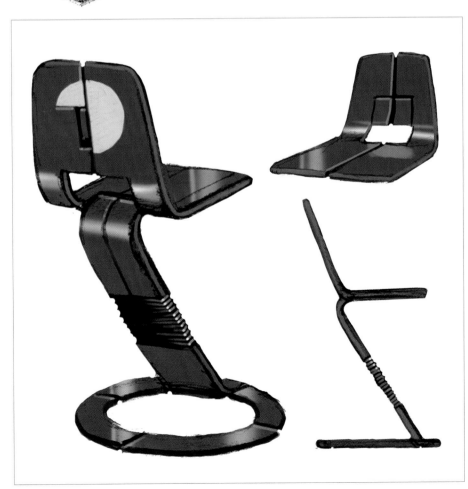

HUMAN HELMETS

One of the most difficult designs turned out to be the human helmets. Because all human armors would share the same basic helmet design and the helmet would frame the characters' faces when they speak in close-ups, it was extremely important that the design was functional and visually appealing.

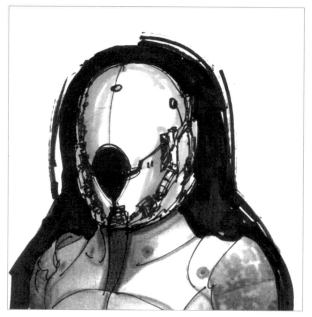

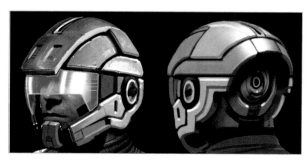

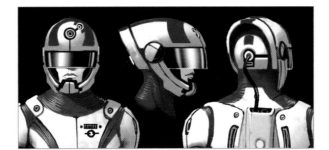

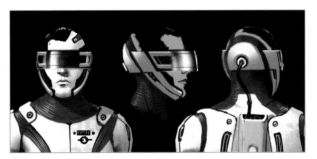

HUMAN HELMETS

To ensure that the characters' faces would be seen even while wearing a helmet, a clear visor and a chin guard that did not obscure the mouth were chosen.

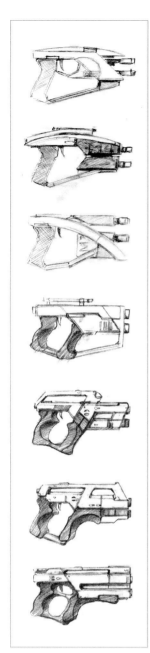

PISTOLS

Numerous variations on pistol designs were developed to find a balance between futuristic design and present-day notions of firepower. To create a look that's unique to Mass Effect, all weapons have two barrels, one atop the other.

GRENADES

Since grenades in Mass Effect can fly in straight lines, they were given a compact disc-like shape.

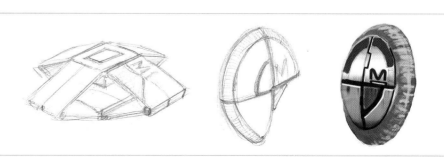

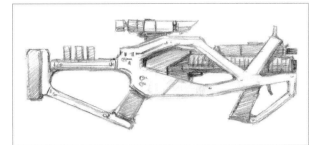

RIFLES

In keeping with Mass Effect's heavy use of circular arcs, the upper body of the rifle is defined by a long curve. While some designs ignored this principle they still applied the double-barrel weapon design (top). The use of arcs is also prominent on the sniper rifle (bottom).

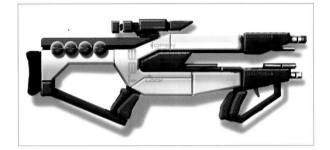

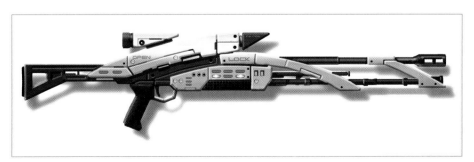

DRONES
AND TURRETS

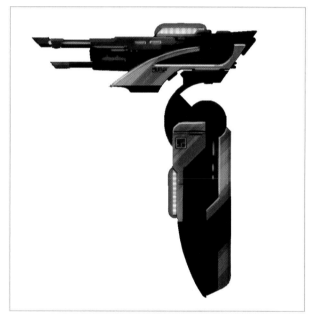

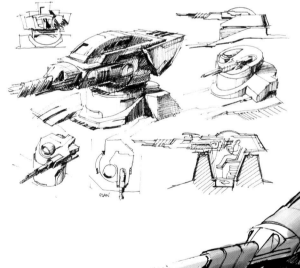

SHOTGUNS

Though the mechanism would work entirely differently in the year 2183, a short-range, scatter-shot weapon was considered to be a valuable weapon for a Spectre's arsenal.

OMNI-TOOL

Designers felt that using technology-based attacks in combat was as important as using conventional weapons. The omni-tool allows characters to manipulate a holographic interface to instantly release these attacks, in addition to activating such non-combat capabilities as hacking electronic locks.

MASS RELAYS

Throwing a starship across the galaxy is no small feat, and Mass Effect's writers and artists had to come up with a believable way to do that. Even after the pseudo-science was worked out, it was still unclear how they would visually realize it. Some ideas for mass relays were elaborate and mechanical, while others were more monolithic.

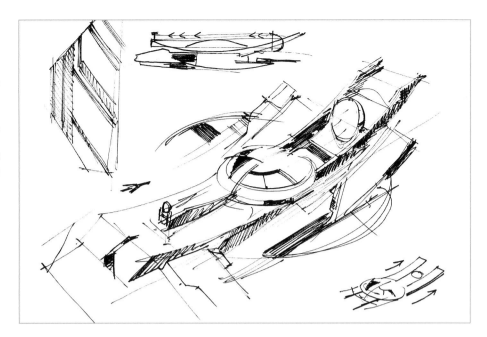

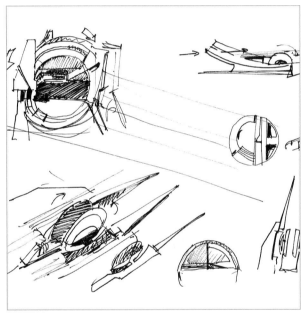

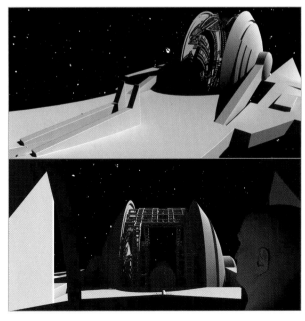

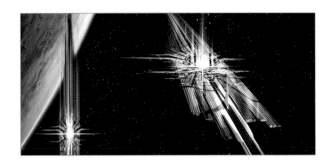

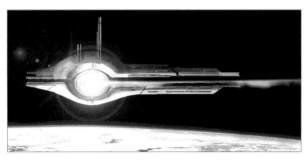

MASS RELAYS

The final design used heavy rotating rings to create the sensation of building power. Its tuning-fork shape appeared to focus the tremendous energy into a straight beam that could project a starship many light-years across the galaxy.

ALIEN WORLDS

In giving players a galaxy of places to explore, Mass Effect required the design of countless alien landscapes and architectural styles. The earliest concepts simply helped the team understand the basic style and format of the game itself. As the story developed, however, specific locations–such as the spectacular space station known as the Citadel–could be developed in great detail. Many of the early production paintings established the look of areas as they are seen in the final game, but as these images illustrate, the entire mood of some areas continued to change until very late in production.

EARLY CONCEPTS

These paintings were done at the very beginning of the project, to help visualize the combat experience of Mass Effect. Though neither of these areas were built as shown, they established an overall style that can be seen throughout Mass Effect.

EARLY CONCEPTS
Even before the initial story outline was written, these early paintings explored ideas for interesting science fiction-inspired locations. In some cases, they inspired the design for planets that would eventually be built for Mass Effect.

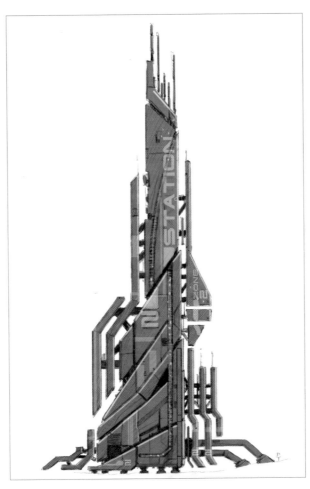

EDEN PRIME

In the first concepts, the human colony of Eden Prime was shown in its natural state, with rolling green hills of farmland. This scheme was used for developing early prototypes of Mass Effect (below). As it became necessary to set a darker tone at the beginning of the story, colors on this planet shifted to a red palette with burning embers raining from the sky.

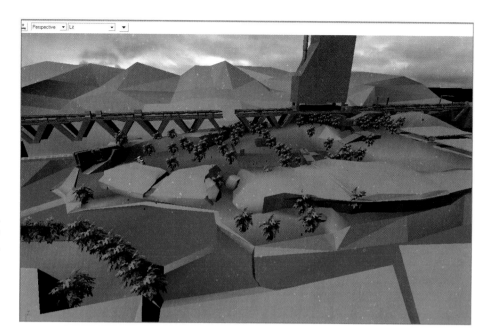

EDEN PRIME

Early layouts featured a tall bridge that transferred cargo between enormous towers. While this bridge was eventually removed, the final version of Eden Prime would still involve a cargo train.

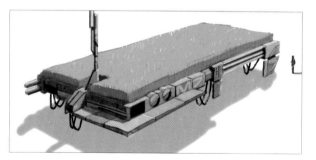

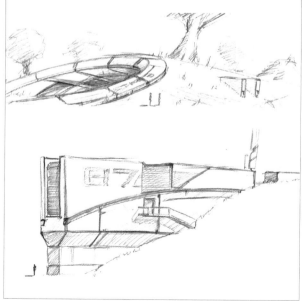

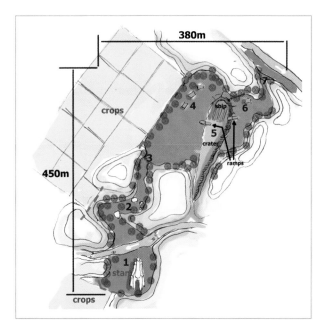

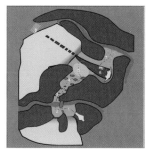

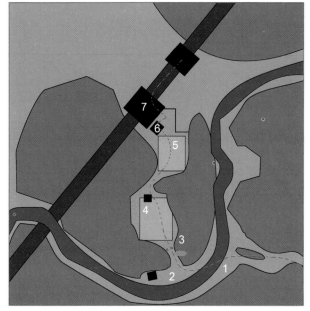

EDEN PRIME

In this "after" shot, it's clear how much damage has been done to the planet by the arrival of Sovereign. The sky is clogged with smoke and entire buildings sheared in half. On the ground, the enormous ships' powerful engines have left a huge circle of burning crops.

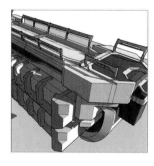

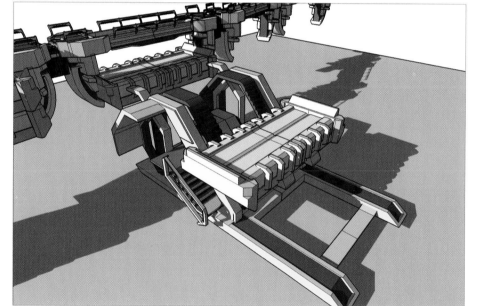

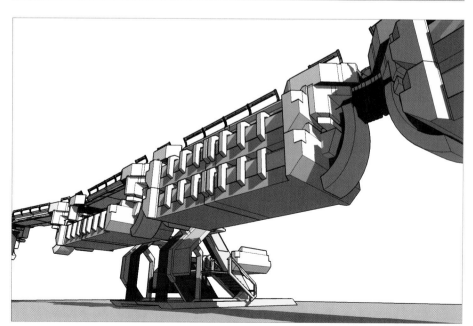

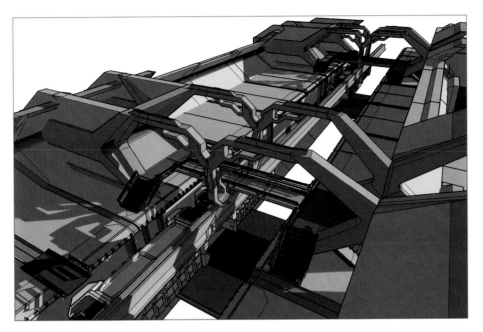

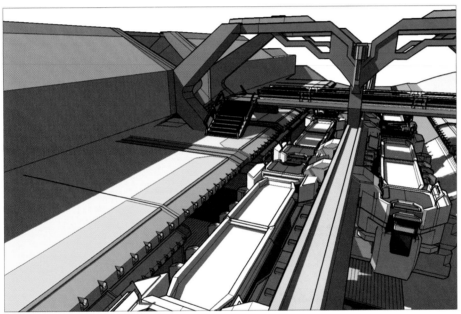

EDEN PRIME TRAIN STATION

This complex structure would not only have to appear functional, but also offer useful combat positions for the fight that would take place there.

THERUM
MINING COMPLEX

n early story drafts, Therum
had a mining facility with a
wide atrium (above), com-
plete with a seedy bar.

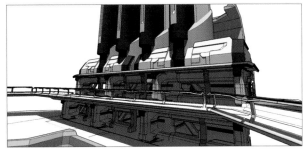

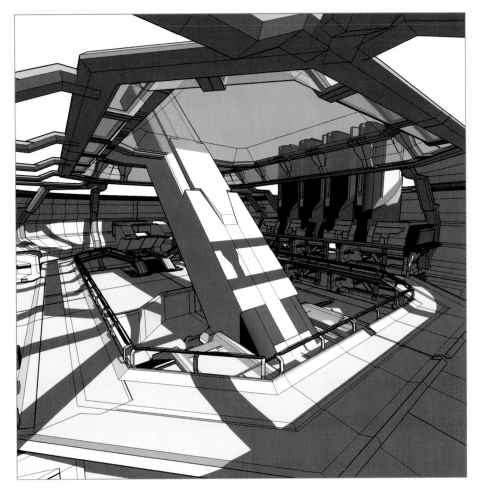

THERUM MINES
While much of the mining equipment was actually used in Mass Effect, some of the interiors were ultimately not required by the story.

THERUM MINES

Silos and gatehouses created a sense of heavy industry on Therum.

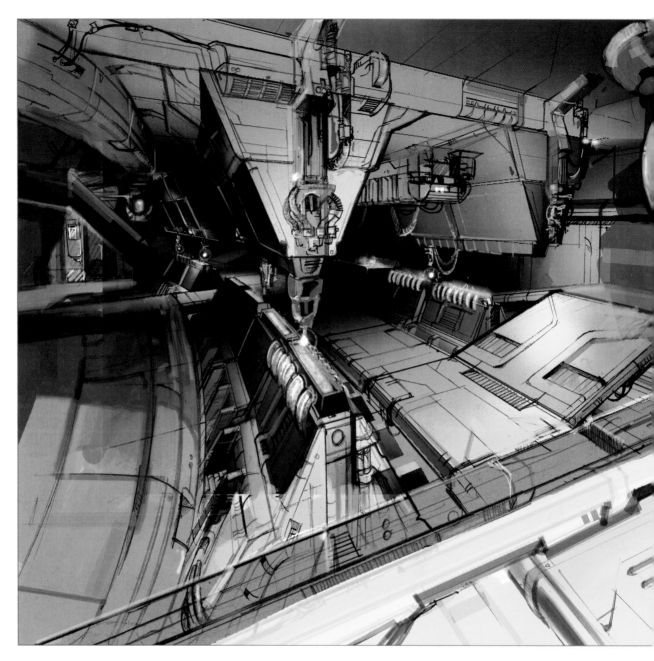

MINING EQUIPMENT

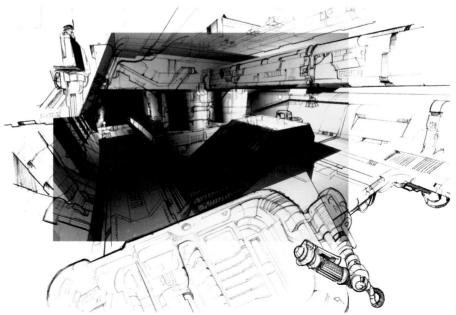

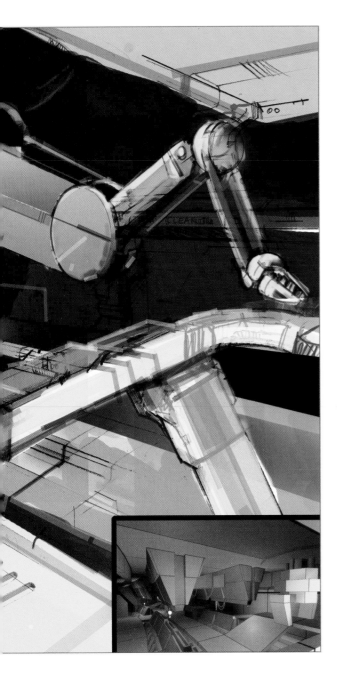

PROTHEAN RUINS

Liara is discovered inside a huge, long-buried Prothean tower. Only part of it was excavated, revealing its tremendous size.

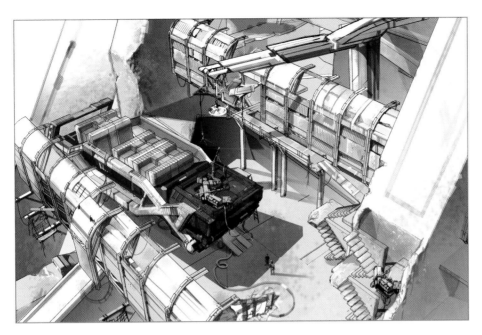

FEROS

A small human colony amid the ancient ruins of a Prothean city, its combination of architectural styles with a destroyed look was particularly difficult to lock down.

THORIAN LAIR

Living beneath the human colony, the gigantic Thorian hangs from the ruins on long tentacles (opposite).

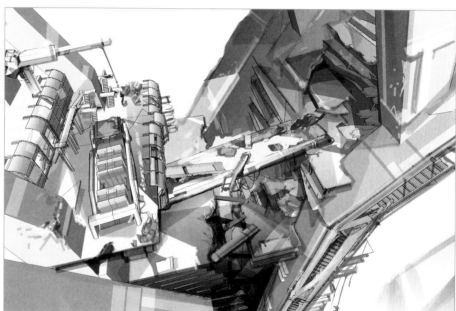

FEROS

These rough 3-D models illustrate the complexity of this world. With rubble and debris forming much of the environment, it was a challenge to ensure that players would know where they were, and where they needed to go.

FEROS

While rough 3-D models helped sort out geometric problems for areas like the Thorian lair, materials and lighting were applied to portions of the level to lock down a final "look." The reflective foil that lines the walls is presumably the remains of ancient insulation, but was inspired by the gold foil that covers many real-life spacecraft.

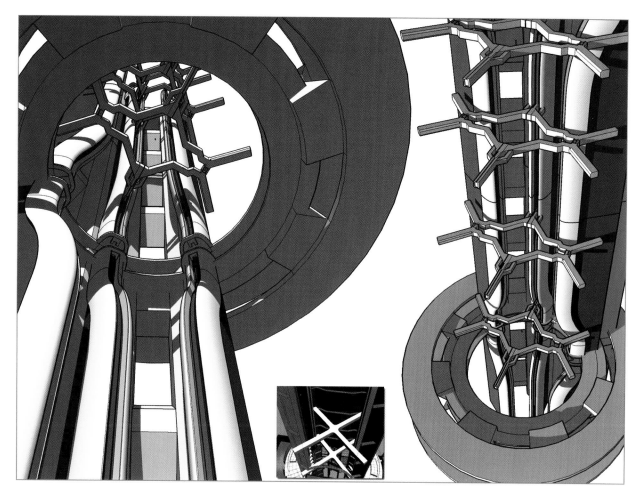

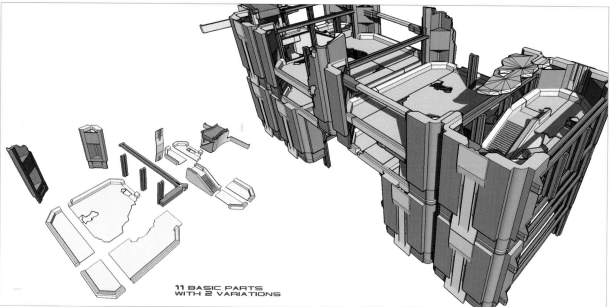

**11 BASIC PARTS
WITH 2 VARIATIONS**

FEROS

Despite its irregular appearance, much of Feros was made with re-usable parts, making it easier to build and less demanding on memory. To test re-usability, the parts were first modeled and assembled in a blocky form.

FEROS

As the 3-D level art took shape, it continued to bear a strong resemblance to the initial painted concept of Feros (below). Later, the artists pushed for an ever higher visual quality, while the color palette shifted into a high-contrast blue-grey scheme.

ILOS

Throughout most of Mass Effect's development, Ilos was a lush jungle world, an idyllic planet whose Prothean inhabitants had long since vanished (above). But as the setting for the dark beginning to the third act of the story, it needed a more ominous feel.

ILOS

These early 3-D models of the environment show the development of the Prothean aqueducts and the Archive. The near-final color scheme (bottom) makes use of dried and twisted vines, as well as an orange color palette with green mid-tones that makes the area feel unsettling and "dead."

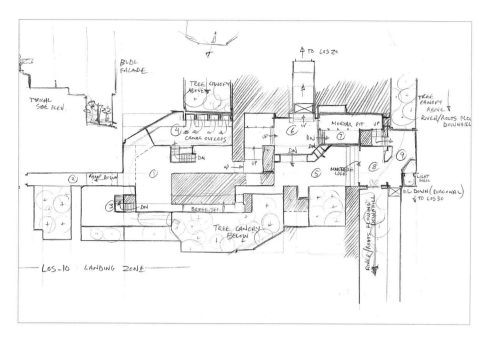

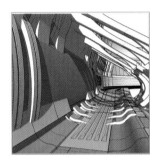

ILOS ARCHIVE

The Archive housed the bodies of thousands of Protheans in suspended animation. Though they were to be awakened when rescued, no rescue occurred. This area was meant to simultaneously capture a sense of wondrous scale and deep sadness.

NOVERIA

Initial designs for Noveria were heavily inspired by the idea of a spaceport in the Swiss Alps. But as the story became more detailed, the snowstorm was intensified and the wooden materials were changed to exposed concrete to create a colder, isolated feeling.

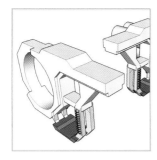

NOVERIA

Though the structures of Noveria were planned in great detail, they were rearranged several times to optimize the story and combat.

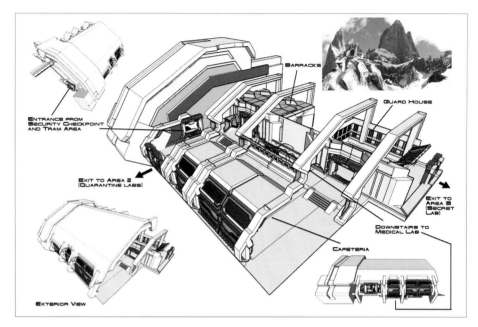

BARRACKS

GUARD HOUSE

ENTRANCE FROM SECURITY CHECKPOINT AND TRAM AREA

EXIT TO AREA 2 (QUARANTINE LABS)

EXIT TO AREA 3 (SECRET LAB)

DOWNSTAIRS TO MEDICAL LAB

CAFETERIA

EXTERIOR VIEW

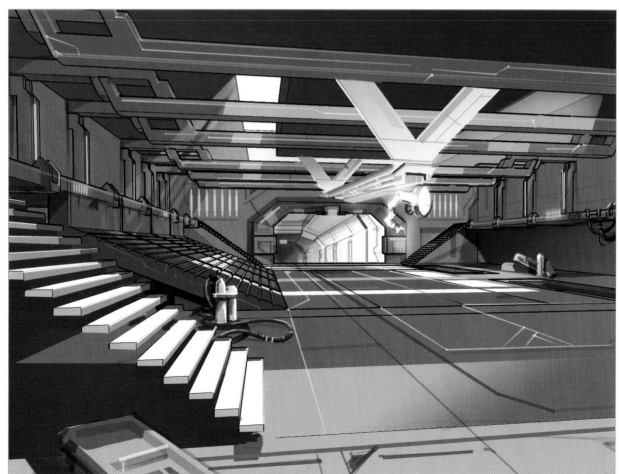

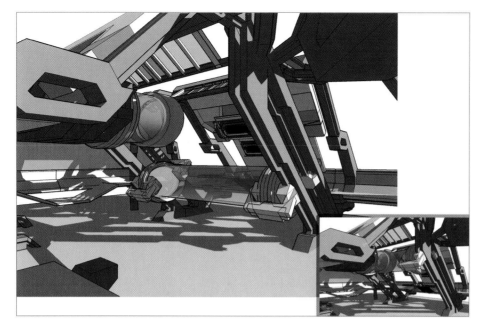

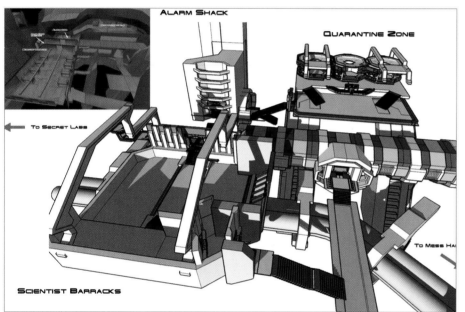

ALARM SHACK

QUARANTINE ZONE

TO SECRET LABS

TO MESS HALL

SCIENTIST BARRACKS

NOVERIA

Early concepts for the Mira
computer (above) and a
generic hallway section
(right). Even though many
of the locations on Noveria
are underground, the hall-
ways feature windows that
reveal the dim blue glow of
the icy cavern walls outside.

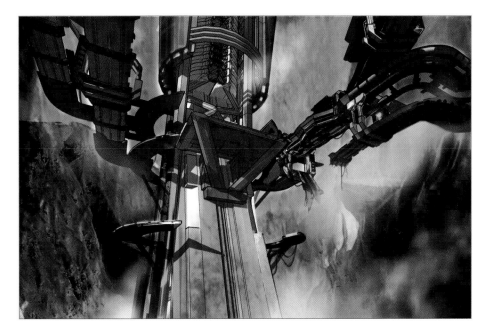

NOVERIA
These early screenshots show the development of the ice and wall materials that would eventually give Noveria its unique look.

THE CITADEL
-PRESIDIUM

The Presidium was inspired by a classic idea from science fiction: the ring-shaped space station. In Mass Effect, this circular environment blends sleek architecture with natural features, such as trees and a winding shoreline, where the political elite of the galaxy can discuss matters of the highest importance. High above, a holographic sky completes the "outdoors" feel.

THE CITADEL

Whereas the Presidium has an open and airy feeling, other areas of the Citadel are more cramped, resembling city streets and office buildings.

THE CITADEL
-APARTMENTS

Although this area was never
built, this painting captured
the cosmopolitan lifestyle
that would be enjoyed by
those who live and work
on the Citadel.

THE CITADEL
-DOCKING BAYS

With a sheet of energy holding the air inside these large bays, the entire Citadel can be seen beyond the docking arm in a stunning vista. These rough 3-D models helped work out the angles and dimensions that would allow the Normandy to approach while showing off this amazing view.

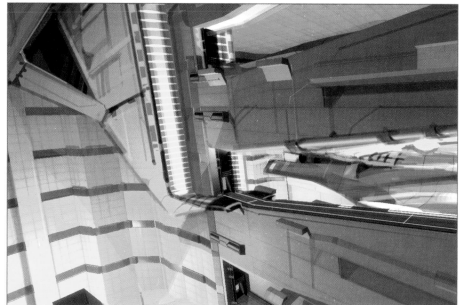

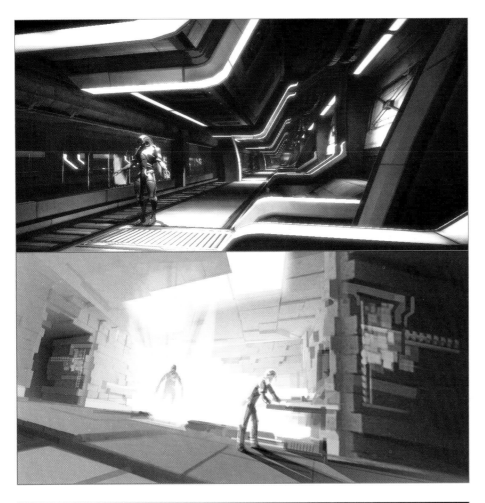

THE CITADEL

A large number of different architectural schemes had to be developed to provide opportunities for exploring the Citadel's diverse locations.

THE CITADEL-EXTERIOR

Though it wasn't always needed, it was useful to know how the entire structure worked, including how the joints moved when it folded into its defensive shell, and how transportation systems would carry millions of citizens around the Citadel.

THE CITADEL-PRESIDIUM TOWER
At the center of the Citadel, the Presidium Tower holds
the pinnacle of galactic power: the Citadel Council (left).

THE CITADEL

Marker renders (top)
established the basic
structural shapes while 3-D
models allowed final
materials and colors to
be defined (bottom).

THE CITADEL

Whereas both the Presidium and Council areas used a limited color palette, the "grungier" areas of the station used saturated colors and high-contrast lighting to capture the feel of a city at night.

VIRMIRE

Inspired by the uniquely-shaped islands of Palau, Virmire is the location of Saren's oceanfront fortress. The combination of white-painted concrete, lush tropical vegetation, and stormy skies creates a memorable atmosphere for the assault that leads players through a series of important revelations.

VIRMIRE

Painted-over screenshots of blocky versions of the level, these concepts helped artists define the details, lighting, and materials that would eventually be added (middle, right). Even though these quickly-drawn paintings lack color, the mood of each area is strongly portrayed.

MASS EFFECT ARTBOOK

VIRMIRE

For each different type of area, artists created an entirely new set of materials and details. For Virmire, rusted metals and weathered paint were applied to structures, while detailed railings, steps, and cable anchors were built for this tropical location.

ACKNOWLEDGEMENTS

The concept art that is the focus of this book was produced by the following artists, without whom this unique vision of the future would not have been possible.

Derek Watts

Matthew Rhodes

Sung Kim

Adrien Cho

Fran Gaulin

Mike Spalding

Mike Trottier

Michael Jeffrey

Sasha Beliaev

Mike Higgins